Harvey Wasserman and Bob Fitrakis

IMPRISON
George W. Bush

Commentary on Why the President Must Be Indicted

THE EMPIRE'S NEW CLOTHES

Harvey Wasserman and Bob Fitrakis

IMPRISON
George W. Bush
Commentary on Why the President Must Be Indicted

With illustrations by Kirk Anderson,
Matt Bors, Rand Careaga,
Donald Guess, Jr., and Matt Wyatt

Published by
HarveyWasserman.com

A Columbus Institute for Contemporary
Journalism book

Imprison George W. Bush:
Commentary on Why the President Must Be Indicted

CICJ Books: freepress.org

The Columbus Institute for Contemporary Journalism is a 501(C)3
Organization.

ISBN: 0-9753402-5-5

Dedicated to
Ray Charles, Dave Dellinger,
Pete Seeger, and Paul Wellstone

Table of contents

FITRAKIS

Why George W. Bush must be tried as a war criminal

The new revelations in Bob Woodward's book, *Plan of Attack*, provide further evidence to convict President George W. Bush of war crimes.

As one of the 49 original signers of the UN Charter, the United States committed itself to the ideals and practices of the norms of international law. Only two U.S. senators voted against the treaty, which includes Article 2(4) that specifically prohibits "...the threat or use of force against the territorial integrity or political independence of any state...." In a September 23, 2003 speech to the United Nations, President Bush noted that both the UN Charter and American founding documents "recognize a moral law that stands above men and nations, which must be defended and enforced by men and nations." Following World War II, just such action was taken at the Nuremberg trials and American, British, French and Soviet jurists established Article VI of the Nuremberg Charter, which legally defines "Crimes Against Peace."

To commit a crime against peace, one must engage in "planning, preparation, initiation or waging of war of aggression, or a war in violation of international treaties . . . or participation in a common plan or conspiracy . . . to wage an aggressive war." Bush is guilty on all these counts. The most damning evidence coming not from the liberal left, but in a series of well-documented books providing revelations by people in his own administration or party. Now, with Woodward's work, the President is condemned with his own words.

Author Ron   Susskind's book about former Bush Treasury Secretary Paul O'Neill, *The Price of Loyalty*, reveals that from the very beginning of the Bush administration, the President was plotting and conspiring to wage aggressive war against Iraq. In *Against All Enemies*, Bush's counter-terrorism expert, Richard Clarke, not only confirmed O'Neill's account of the Bush administration's obsession with attacking Iraq, yet also shows us an insider's view on the illegal planning, preparation and initiation of the war through the deliberate manipulation of intelligence. President Nixon's strategist, Kevin Phillips, documents four generations of war profiteering and deception by the Bush/Walker clan in *American Dynasty*.

Finally, in the latest blockbuster, Pulitzer Prize-winning Watergate reporter Bob Woodward outlines Bush's illegal attack plan. Woodward establishes that five days after 9/11, the President was secretly scheming to go after, not bin Laden – the man responsible for the 9/11 attack – but rather bin Laden's arch enemy Saddam Hussein. Specifically, 72 days after 9/11, Bush gave Defense Secretary Donald Rumsfeld the orders to draw up the secret war plans. Once enacted, these plans made George W. Bush a war criminal, just like the Nazi generals at Nuremberg.

Bush, supported by the mainstream corporate media, has hidden behind the semantics of "pre-emption." Under international law, a pre-emptive strike is allowed when a nation is preparing for an imminent attack. Bush would be hard pressed before any tribunal, short of a Texas kangaroo court, to establish that the Iraqi military was an imminent threat to the U.S. Iraq was a defeated, heavily impoverished nation, under economic sanctions and restricted by U.S.-enforced no-fly zones in both its north and south.

The so-called "Bush doctrine" is in reality an echo of the illegal Nazi doctrine of "preventive" war, which asserted that any country that may pose a future non-specific threat can be attacked and occupied. This is not "higher moral law," rather it is a repugnant Nazi doctrine last heard when Germany attacked Poland prior to World War II.

Add to the mounting evidence against Bush's criminality the fact that his key advisors are the likes of Paul Wolfowitz and Richard Perle, who have been publicly waging a campaign to attack Iraq since the end of the first Gulf War in 1991. A quick visit to the Project for a New American Century website establishes their blatant disregard for both the UN Charter and Nuremberg principles. Their neocon or vulcan ideology draws in part from renegade Trotskyist Max Shachtman's belief that authoritarian regimes are incapable of reform. Thus, they adopt the rhetoric of human rights hawks – painting any conflict as a clash between "freedom and tyranny" – to resurrect discredited Nazi war doctrines. Even the ever-cautious Columbus *Dispatch* recently editorialized that Bush is a "militant unilateralist" and attributes the President's rhetoric and worldview to the "Vulcans."

Woodward's book reads, as do Clarke's and Susskind's, as another lengthy prosecutory indictment against the Bush administration. Bush's only defense against such blatant illegality is to find the real or imagined, or more likely recently planted, weapons of mass destruction in Iraq. For the last two months the Mehr News Agency from Tehran, Iran has reported allegations that the U.S. and British governments have been unloading weapons of mass destruction into southern Iraq. The news service claims that these weapons are dismantled Soviet-era nuclear material and weapons. Reuters reported these allegations as well. The President's recent comments that he hasn't given up on finding weapons of mass destruction, sound eerily familiar to his refrain in Florida on Election Eve, when he was asked if he was going to concede the election when exit polls showed him losing. He told the media that his brother Jeb's political forces on the ground were indicating different results. What are Bush's forces on the ground in Iraq doing now, particularly his private contractor friends?

For a President who took us into war under an illegal Nazi doctrine and sold it to the American people based on cooked intelligence information, would it not be the next step to simply plant the evidence he needs amidst the chaos of a disintegrating Iraq? With the illusion of Iraqi sovereignty fading and potential disaster looming with a premature turnover, Bush's re-election bid may be based on his hitting another "trifecta": "capturing" Osama bin Laden, "trying" Saddam Hussein, and "finding" weapons of mass destruction. The recent alarmist talk about another terrorist attack prior to the election should be cause for great concern for an administration that conveniently ignored the overwhelming evidence of the Al Qaeda attack.

News services worldwide must stop the madness of George the Lesser, who was as ill-prepared to accept dynastic succession as the infamous Ethelred the Unready. Historians of the British monarchy suggest that the term "Unready" should be read as the archaic British term "redeless" meaning "without counsel." Thus, Ethelred, like George the Lesser, made mistakes by impulsively pursuing action without wise counsel. Thankfully, the wisest of Bush's former counsels are warning the people this election year. The people of the United States need to hear their warnings and constitute an international People's Tribunal to try President Bush for the war crimes he is committing.

April 20, 2004

EXPANSION OF THE PRE-EMPTIVE WAR DOCTRINE

WASSERMAN

Put George W. Bush in prison!!!

Those American soldiers torturing and sexually abusing Iraqi prisoners have made criminals of us all.

And there are only two possible responses to this horrible outrage: get out of Iraq. Now!

And imprison the man responsible, George W. Bush.

Any fantasy that the United States could "bring democracy" or inject stability or somehow do something praiseworthy for the Iraqi people irrevocably died with the publication of those photographs.

With Bush, the flow of abominations only seems to deepen and get worse with every passing day. Any whining or carping that he is not personally responsible is pure hypocrisy. This man belongs in prison!

Every serious Iraqi, Arab or Islamic leader, commentator or "person in the street" has said the same thing: "Game Over". The Americans must leave.

All further blood spilled in Iraq is senseless, useless, gratuitous slaughter.

All killing is only further insult to the people of that tortured nation and to the Americans sent there to kill and be killed. The only question now is: "who will be the last person to die for this mistake?"

And when will the person most responsible, George W. Bush,

pay for this abomination?

Thanks to Bush, we Americans---all of us---will forever be seen in much of the world's eyes as parties to torture and forced sexual abuse and a cynical Christian crusade whose idea of religious conversion apparently involves rape or a photographic facsimile.

As Americans, we are duty-bound to hold the guilty parties responsible, and there is ultimately one party to point to: the President of the United States.

As always, Bush takes no personal responsibility. His radio rodents like Rush Limbaugh say the photos were fake. That Bush couldn't have known about any of this. That those reports circulating for weeks about widespread torture and abuse in the Iraqi prisons---not to mention an unknown number of apparent murders---could not have been seen by Bush, and therefore he was not responsible.

Well, where does the buck stop?

It was on Bush's watch that the attacks on the World Trade Center killed 3000 people. He spent the weeks leading up to the attack on vacation, ignoring briefings about its likelihood.

The 9/11 attacks were funded and planned through Saudi Arabia, with whose leaders Bush has close personal ties.

The attack on Iraq was almost entirely Bush's personal doing. He meaningfully consulted only a tiny handful of neo-conservative fanatics. He discussed it with a Saudi oil prince before his own Secretary of State.

In all US history there has been no act of war more the product of a single individual than this one.

Bush consciously and systematically lied to Congress, the UN and the world to get the war going.

By all accounts, Saddam Hussein and the Iraqis had nothing to do with 9/11. Bush attacked anyway, making a mockery of US and UN legal processes.

Bush immediately proclaimed the war a Christian Crusade, and his fundamentalist supporters still see it that way.

Bush shouted to the world that the Iraqis had weapons of mass destruction. He lied.

Bush's ventriloquist, Dick Cheney, said the Iraqis would "dance in the streets" with the American victory, but those streets are now soaked in blood. Bush and Cheney's business cronies have grotesquely profited from the ghastly slaughter.

Bush proclaimed "Mission Accomplished" a year ago, but the death toll has soared, and will now soar again.

Bush said resistance would disappear with the capture of Saddam Hussein.

Bush used Saddam's most infamous prison for these acts of torture. Iraqi commentators hated that the Americans left the prison standing at all. Now we find Bush has used it to commit the same crimes Saddam did.

For all this and way too much more, the finger of guilt points just one place: the Oval Office. In the name of a "Higher Father," Bush ordered this attack virtually on his own, and trashed every legal and moral constraint to get it done.

We Americans have a higher responsibility to stop this flood of outrages, and bring this man to justice.

If those photos from Iraq prove anything, it is that George W. Bush must face criminal prosecution as soon as possible.

These abuses taint us all. As Americans, there is just one way to redeem ourselves: get these murderous torturers out of the White House and into a prison of their own, where they belong.

May 5, 2004

WHY DICK TALKS OUT THE SIDE OF HIS MOUTH

FITRAKIS

Why Bush must be captured and tried alongside Saddam Hussein

As the   new year unfolds, one unmistakable fact remains unreported in America's submissive mainstream media: our President George W. Bush is a war criminal. Any attempt to state this obvious fact is ignored and any Democratic Presidential hopeful who suggests we repudiate the new Bush doctrine of American imperialism and instead, work for world peace, is dismissed as a "vanity" candidate and told to drop out of the race.

The case against President Bush is overwhelming. The nonprofit American Society of International Law, consisting mainly of scholars, has laid out the case against the President in article after article in a dispassionate fashion. Following the September 11, 2001 attack on the United States by the Al Qaeda terrorist organization, both the United States and Britain attempted to comply with international law. When Operation Enduring Freedom, the massive military assault on Afghanistan, began on October 7, 2001, both countries adhered to the United Nations Charter Article 51 by notifying the Security Council that they were attacking Afghanistan under the doctrine of individual and collective self-defense. Most international law scholars accepted the United States' right to self-defense against terrorist bases in Afghanistan.

From legitimate self-defense, the Bush administration suddenly resurrected the discredited Nazi doctrine of "preventive war" with Bush and his collaborators arguing that in the battle of "good" versus "evil" the United States had the right to attack any country that might pose a future threat to our nation.

The Bush administration is using the recent capture of Saddam Hussein for propaganda purposes to justify its illegal and criminal war against Iraq. Some newspapers have gone so far to question the practicality of the "Bush doctrine" without pointing out its illegal and criminal nature. For example, Matthew Hay Brown of the Orlando Sentinel wrote in a news analysis piece the day Saddam was captured, that: "By striking at a country that was not threatening to attack the United States and without hard evidence of weapons of mass destruction or links to al-Qaeda officials hope to show the length to which the United States would go to protect itself."

The *Columbus Dispatch* ran Brown's analysis on its front page. Still there was no mention of the universal repudiation of the Bush doctrine.

Let's start with the obvious. Any law scholar will tell you that pre-emptive self-defense is unlawful under international law – from Article VI of the Nuremberg Charter to the UN Charter. In fact, the United States was the guiding force behind both the Nuremberg trials and the establishment of the United Nations. At the end of the second world war, with the Nazis defeated and discredited, the United Nations Charter, a treaty binding on the U.S., prohibited nations using preventive force in Article II, Section 4. Only the Security Council has the authority to take measures against "threats to the peace, breaches of the peace, and acts of aggression."

The only exception to this is the right of individual and collective self-defense that the U.S. and Britain invoked under Article 51. The key, of course, is that you has to be attacked or that an enemy must be in the process of attacking you. Under the UN Charter, you cannot simply say here's a list of "rogue nations" who may at some undefined time in the near future pose a threat to you because they may harbor weapons of mass destruction, which we have in abundance, and they are not allowed to have. Nor is there anything under international law that says simply developing a weapons program amounts to an armed threat or attack. If this were true, every country on Earth would be justified in attacking the U.S., the country with the greatest number of WMD's, at any time.

A few voices in the Democratic Presidential primary have attempted to raise substantial issues concerning U.S. foreign policy but the mainstream media is obsessed with its "politics as horse race" mentality focusing mostly on who is in the lead. So, while the talking heads analyze the post-Saddam capture "Bush bounce" and predict that no President with a favorable rating over 60% going into a presidential election year has ever lost, they miss the point that if they actually reported that world consensus holds their president to be a war criminal, then maybe his rating wouldn't be so high.

Perhaps the most egregious example of a journalist trying to silence debate on the Bush doctrine was ABC debate moderator Ted Koppel who suggested that peace candidates Dennis Kucinich, Ambassador Carol Mosley-Braun and Rev. Al Sharpton should drop out of the debate. When Kucinich directly challenged Koppel suggesting that it wasn't the media's role to define who should be in or out of a presidential race prior to the people casting votes, ABC retaliated by pulling the fulltime reporter covering the Kucinich campaign.

Recently the Pope reminded the world that the war against Iraq is illegal. Perhaps ABC could take the fulltime reporter they pulled from Kucinich and put him on fulltime research on the illegality of the Bush doctrine and its eerie parallels to Nazi Germany and its attack on Poland.

And they might want to look into the story *Popular Mechanics* broke in December 2003 showing a satellite photo of a pipeline through Kuwait looting Iraqi oil from the Ramalah oil field.

December 31, 2003

WASSERMAN

Bush the torturer must leave office

The torture at Al   Ghraib is a direct reflection of George W. Bush's moral character, his political beliefs and his military abilities.

Those images streaming out of Iraq reflect the true face of George W. Bush. Until he resigns or is removed from office, there is no way to begin removing the stain on the American character.

This is not about Donald   Rumsfeld or a few "bad" soldiers in the field. Nor is it merely about "softening up" detainees to extract information about terrorism.

At their core, these outrages are gratuitous and psychotic. They stem directly from the morals and character of the man now occupying the Oval Office. The beheading of a young American represents the inevitable beginning of a horrific blowback. The spin that somehow Bush operatives are above such behavior, and had nothing to do with provoking it, is tragic nonsense.

The ultimate statement was made by Bush himself when he was governor of Texas. The Texas prison system has a tragic history of sadism and brutality. But Bush dragged it to new depths.

Bush was a governor in love with the death penalty. He executed 152 prisoners, more than any other governor in US history.

One was Karla Faye Tucker, for whose death Bush became justly infamous. Tucker was convicted of murder, but in prison underwent a dramatic conversion to the kind of fundamentalist Christianity Bush claims to embrace. She became an astute observer of the prison system, and asked Bush for a meeting. He refused.

After Bush had her killed, he sadistically mocked Karla Faye Tucker on a conservative talk show. Asked what she might have said had he met with her, Bush assumed a scornful whine and imitated a woman pleading for her life. Governor Bush apparently found this as funny as his recent presidential search under a table for the Weapons of Mass Destruction that never were found in Iraq.

As governor, Bush also executed an immigrant who was denied access to representatives of his home country, as required by the Vienna Convention on Consular Relations. The US was a party to that convention. But Bush explained that "Texas did not sign the Vienna Convention, so why should we be subject to it?"

In that spirit Bush scorned the United Nations Convention on the Rights of the Child by joining Saudi Arabia, Iran, Pakistan and Yemen in executing minors. More than 90 percent of the children held on Bush's death row were non-whites.

Because Bush slashed Texas mental health programs, his prisons were full of psychologically impaired victims, whom he also held eligible for execution.

The US military's own *Taguba Report* has described Bush's Iraqi prisons as being rife with "sadistic, blatant and wanton criminal abuses." But they merely reflect conditions in Texas prisons when Bush was governor. According to federal Judge William Wayne Justice, Texas inmates under Bush, like those under him in Iraq, "credibly testified to the existence of violence, rape and extortion in the prison system and about their own suffering from such abysmal conditions." A 1996 videotape shows guards attacking prisoners with stun guns and dogs, then dragging them face-down into their cells. One prisoner with an IQ of 56 died of "natural causes" in his uncooled cell during a brutal 1998 heat wave.

With a thousand civilian prisoners in Afghanistan, perhaps

10,000 in Iraq and hundreds more at Guantanamo, Bush is fighting the International Convention Against Torture. Amnesty International cites "a pattern of physical and verbal abuse by some corrections officers" and abuse of "basic human rights" by Bush's military command, including systematic sleep deprivation. The Red Cross reported such problems as much as a year ago. Independent reports also indicate that the vast majority of Iraqis being abused are not terrorists at all, but merely luckless civilians detained in random, disorganized sweeps.

The gruesome photography from Iraq has apparently been a part of Bush's torture process, meant---where it has any purpose at all--- to shame the prisoners. At least one shot apparently depicts the forcible rape of a young inmate by a guard. Another prisoner has apparently been photographed while being forced to masturbate, an astonishing demand coming from a regime whose party impeached a President of the United States for concealing private, consensual sex.

A primary source of many of these revelations has been investigative reporter Seymour Hersh. Hersh became famous three decades ago for uncovering atrocities at My Lai in Vietnam, which current Secretary of State Colin Powell worked to keep secret.

Powell has since gained new infamy by lying to the world about Weapons of Mass Destruction and Saddam Hussein's alleged attempt to buy uranium for nuclear weapons.

But like My Lai, atrocious behavior in Iraq comes straight from the top. Bush's contempt for international law, including the Geneva Accords, has been legend. His stirring praise for Defense Secretary Rumsfeld must be taken at face value. If Rumsfeld is doing a "superb job," it's because Rumsfeld is doing superbly what George W. Bush wants done.

What Bush did as governor he now does as   president. It has nothing to do with stopping terrorism or protecting the United States. It's not the product of a few "bad" or poorly trained soldiers. It's not about a wayward Secretary of Defense and his out-of-control military apparatus. The inevitable reaction that's now come with this first beheading has been provoked by an administration engaged in global drunk driving.

This ghastly spiral of brutality is all about George W. Bush and who he really is. And since he is doing this in the name of the United States, it is ultimately about us, and what we do about him.

May 12, 2004

...but it wasn't systemic...

FITRAKIS

Torture and abuse: A pattern and practice of the U.S. military

The official word from the Bush administration is that the torture and sexual abuse of Iraqi prisoners by U.S. troops in Iraq's Abu Ghraib prison is not "systematic," according to General Richard Myers, Chairman of the Joint Chiefs of Staff. This type of torture of indigenous and Third World people, however, is well-documented as a pattern and practice of the U.S. military and the CIA.

In January 1997, the Baltimore Sun exposed a 1983 CIA torture manual that was used to instruct five Latin American nations' security forces. The infamous disclaimer in the torture manual read: "While we do not stress the use of coercive techniques, we want to make you aware of them and the proper way to use them." A 1996 U.S. government investigation into the U.S. Army School of the Americas in Ft. Benning, Georgia resulted in the release of no less than seven training manuals used at the school "which taught murder, torture, and extortion" as a means of repressing so-called "subversives," according to a Congressional report. In addition to the seven training manuals, add the 1983 Honduran

Interrogation Manual and the 1984 Contra Manual as evidence of the U.S. military industrial complex's long-standing practice of torture.

Recall the comments of former CIA Station Chief and National Security Council Coordinator John Stockwell about the CIA Contra Manual and actions promoted by the U.S. military in Nicaragua: "They go into villages. They haul out families. With the children forced to watch, they castrate the father. They peel the skin off his face. They put a grenade in his mouth, and pull the pin. With the children forced to watch, they gang-rape the mother, and slash her breasts off. And sometimes, for variety they make the parents watch while they do these things to the children."

In his lecture, "The Secret Wars of the CIA,"   Stockwell outlined in detail the use of sexual humiliation from his own investigation. "She told about being tortured one day: She's on this table, naked in a room full of six men and they're doing these incredibly painful, degrading things to her body. There's an interruption. The American is called to the telephone, and he's in the next room, and the others take a smoke break. She's lying on this table, and he's saying: 'Oh, hi Honey. Yes, I can wrap it up here in another hour or so, and meet you and the kids at the Ambassador's on the way home.'"

The recent Iraqi allegations of sexual humiliation, forcing simulated sex, forcing detainees to "publicly masturbate" and at least one charge of an interrogator raping a male prisoner, according to the *Guardian U.K.*, simply are a continuation of condoned U.S. military/CIA practices.

By now much of the world has seen images of a hooded Iraqi prisoner with electrical wires attached to his body. This is another long-standing practice of U.S. military and CIA interrogators. The Baltimore Sun also uncovered a 1963 manual called "KUBARK Counterintelligence Interrogation" containing references to the use of "electric shock." CIA spokesperson Mark Mansfield told the Sun in 1997 that the agency was now opposed to the use of such torture tactics. The discovery of the KUBARK document did little to prompt a full-scale investigation into U.S. military/CIA techniques, and if they were promoted throughout the world.

Stockwell and others have tried to remind America of the use of electronic torture by Dan Mitrione, the notorious U.S. "policy advisor" killed in 1970 in Uruguay. Stockwell claims that Mitrone perfected the use of an ultra-thin highly conductive wire that could be hooked to hand-cranked field phones and inserted as a catheter to shock subversives. A.J. Langguth wrote about this in a July 11, 1979 New York Times article entitled "Torture's Teachers."

Langguth notes in his article that "… the C.I.A. sent an operative to teach interrogation methods to SAVAK, the Shah's secret police, [and] that the training included instructions in torture, and the techniques were copied from the Nazis."

The only new trend in pattern and practice of U.S. military/CIA torture interrogation is the strong push to privatization, in line with President Bush's ideology. The Guardian U.K. reports that both CACI International Inc. and Titan Corporations were names involved in the Abu Ghraib prison operation.

CACI's website offers the following insight on the for-profit organization. Its goal is to "Help America's intelligence community collect, analyze, and share global information in the war on terrorism." The late CIA Director William Casey's dream was the complete privatization of covert, and usually illegal, operations. In part, this privatization was used during the Iran-Contra affair through the likes of Richard Secord's Enterprise. By privatizing, they seek to subvert the Geneva Conventions on war and other universal standards of human rights.

The torture and sexual humiliation of Iraqi prisoners is merely another sad and well-documented chapter of a pompous nation using virtuous rhetoric while perpetuating obvious evils. The fact that the U.S. military, with for-profit contractors, is torturing Iraqis in Saddam's former prisons while claiming to bring American, and Bush's, values to the war devastated nation is an irony not lost on the world.

The Bush administration is committed to systematically destroying the Iraqis in order to liberate them. The United Nations must demand that the people of the United States form a Truth

Commission to look deeply and honestly into the practices of its bloated military and security industrial complexes. The truth may yet set Americans free.

May 4, 2004

WASSERMAN

Will Bush the Beheader use terrorism to become America's Pinochet?

Will George W. Bush use terrorism to become America's Pinochet?

Attorney-General John Ashcroft is priming the public for a terrorist attack, which can only mean Bush is sharpening his blades to behead the Constitution.

Augusto Pinochet seized absolute power in Chile on September 11, 1973. The US national security apparatus, including George H.W. Bush, used terrorism as an excuse to help Pinochet destroy what had been a constitutional democracy.

So is Shrub a president? Or is he a Pinochet?

By a 4:1 margin American historians have already rated W. "a failure." More than one in ten surveyed in the recent George Mason University History News Network Poll also rate Bush as "the worst president ever."

But ultimately, this Bush has no peer among US presidents. Let's look at three likely matches.

Richard Nixon trained Dick Cheney and Karl Rove as Dirty Tricksters. Nixon is Bush's role model for corruption, cynicism and personal psychosis. But Nixon was also a skilled, literate global diplomat who opened doors to China and the former Soviet Union and supported environmental protection. Bush has trashed all that.

Herbert Hoover callously presided over the beginnings of America's worst economic depression. Bush is right there. But Hoover was also a skilled, literate bureaucrat, and a Quaker-raised foe of war. Not exactly Bush.

Warren G. Harding was astonishingly corrupt. Bush, Halliburton and Enron have more than matched him. But Harding also hated repression and brought the anti-war socialist Eugene V. Debs straight from a federal prison cell to meet him in the Oval Office. Bush might well have had Debs executed.

Ultimately, Bush's real peers are not US presidents but Third World dictators, like Pinochet, many of whom his father also put in office. Their coda is clear:

- Use of "terror" as an excuse for totalitarian control;
- Official secrecy for its own sake;
- Seizure of power in contempt of free elections;
- Totalitarian militarism;
- Abuse of human rights and liberties;
- Love of the death penalty;
- Hatred of a free press;
- Imprisonment without legal recourse;
- Widespread torture;
- Brazen theft of public billions;
- "Free market" smokescreens for corporate domination;
- Taxing the poor to benefit the rich;
- Hatred of labor unions;
- Decimation of the natural environment;
- Assaulting elected leaders anywhere, anytime;
- Contempt for international treaties;
- Reactionary alliance with right wing church groups;
- Contempt for women's rights;
- Manipulating divisions of race and class.

The one American actually offered a dictatorship, George Washington, turned it down, shaping the nature of the Presidency for more than two centuries....until now.

Meanwhile Bush has beheaded the American economy, replacing First World surpluses with Third World debt.

Reminiscent of Joe Stalin, foreign intelligence, economic assessment and even basic science must not contradict Rovian spin or fundamentalist prophecy.

American education, once the envy of the world, is in shambles, with global students now turning away for the first time. America's moral prestige, never higher than after September 11, 2001, has been trashed. No US president has ever been so personally hated.

And never has a would-be Third World dictator stood more ready to shred our Constitution.

Stalin once quipped that power resides not with those who cast the votes, but with those that count them.

Bush may try to follow Stalin's (and brother   Jeb's) lead by stealing the 2004 election, as in 2000. Or he may try to seize power like Pinochet did on 9/11/73 in a repressive crusade against convenient terrorism.

But one thing is certain: if Shrub's hyped-up power play succeeds, the beheading of America will be complete.

May 28, 2004

WASSERMAN & FITRAKIS

Did Ashcroft 'behead' an innocent man in an Ohio election-terror scam?

While the major media screams about the latest beheading in the Middle East, John Ashcroft's destruction of a man in the Middle West -- likely for political purposes -- has gone unnoticed.

The ghastly court appearance here in Columbus, Ohio, of Nuradin Abdi has underscored the high likelihood that the Bush Administration used variations of torture to break this impoverished Somali immigrant. And his dubious indictment may well have been used to overshadow a campaign visit here by John Kerry. No Republican has ever won the White House without carrying Ohio.

On Monday, June 14, the eve of Kerry's two-day visit here, Attorney-General Ashcroft dramatically seized national headlines by unsealing a month-old four-count indictment of Abdi, a Somali native living in Columbus. "The American heartland was targeted for death and destruction by an al-Qaeda cell allegedly which included a Somali immigrant who will now face justice," Ashcroft boasted.

Ashcroft failed to point out that Abdi had been in custody since

November 28, 2003. Federal investigators claim Abdi allegedly bragged that he wanted to blow up a mall. But according to CBSNEWS.com, "no specific mall was targeted. No explosives were in hand. And it was unclear that the alleged terrorist had the wherewithal to do it."

Abdi faces up to 80 years in prison and $1 million in fines. According to U.S. immigration records, Abdi first entered the United States in 1995, resided in Canada, then re-entered the U.S. in August 1997. Official statements say the US granted Abdi asylum as a refugee in January 1999 after Abdi gave false information to immigration officials. His November 2003 arrest was on immigration charges. He has been held in prison under extremely dubious circumstances.

He was not formally charged with terrorism. His family could not see him and heard little from him. He had no legal representation.

Last week Ashcroft charged Abdi with plotting to blow up an unnamed shopping mall in central Ohio. The super-hyped "findings" immediately followed embarrassing new revelations about the administration's use of torture, and came just before John Kerry's campaign appearance in the capitol of this crucial swing state. Kerry raised a record $2 million in his two days here.

Ashcroft says that while in prison Nuradin Abdi claimed to have gone to Mecca on a pilgrimage but instead went to Ethiopia for terrorist training. In a BBC interview, Abdi's brother, Abdiaziz, said "Nuradin has not been to Ethiopia. He hasn't been to Mecca, either."

Federal Magistrate Mark Abel ordered Abdi transferred to a federal psychiatric facility to determine if he is mentally competent. The evidence used to determine Magistrate Abel's decision remains sealed.

Here's how ABC's Peter Jennings described the public announcement of Abdi's indictment: "In Washington today, the Attorney General said that al-Qaeda has been planning to blow up a shopping mall in Ohio. John Ashcroft went before the cameras to say that a man from Somalia, currently in U.S. custody, is at the heart of this plan. Over the last three years Mr. Ashcroft has made several dramatic announcements about terrorist plots in the U.S. and it's hard to verify them because the evidence is held in such secrecy."

In court, Abdi looked nothing like a terrorist -- or his former self. His family and the larger Somali community here were horrified to see Abdi enter the courtroom smiling vacantly and failing to recognize his own brother. Apparently unconscious of his surroundings, Abdi banged his head repeatedly on a table and grinned at nothing. Many who know Abdi in the central Ohio community say the vague, sensational charges against him are absurdly out of character.

No photos have emerged of abuse in prison. But Abdi's new attorney, his family and the community who knew him find little else to conclude. Some say he has apparently lost his mind under the conditions of his incarceration.

The four-count indictment returned by a federal grand jury in Columbus centers around charges that Abdi conspired with Lyman Faris and others to blow up an unidentified shopping mall. Faris is serving 20 years in prison for allegedly planning (but taking no actual action) to sabotage the Brooklyn Bridge.

Faris's family says he's had a long-standing struggle with mental difficulties. Faris was held in prison for several months before suddenly being fingered as a high-profile terrorist. The Bush Administration says Faris visited the Brooklyn Bridge and tried to buy equipment to aid an alleged al-Qaeda attack.

Faris and Abdi attended the same mosque in Columbus. Home to more than 30,000 Somalis, this is the second-largest Somali community in the US after Minneapolis.

The Somali community here has met en masse about the Abdi indictment. It has been quick to point out the mistake the government made in the November 8, 2001 world headlines touting a Bush crackdown on financial networks allegedly tied to Osama bin Laden . Among those arrested in a much-hyped Columbus raid was Somali businessman Hassan Hussein, owner of Barakaat Enterprise Inc., a financial transfer business. At the end of August 2002, the U.S. Treasury Department quietly removed Hussein and two other Somali individuals from its list of alleged supporters of terrorism and dropped all charges against them.

Hussein's lawyer, Kevin O'Brien, told reporters after the charges were dropped that "I wish the government would just come out and say, 'We screwed up' and apologize. For ten months we asked them to produce proof, and not once did they produce a shred of information."

Somali expert Ted   Dagne of the Congressional Research Service in Washington, D.C. called the government's decision to close down Barakaat "a major blunder" based on "junk intelligence." The BBC reported that 60% of all Somalians use Barakaat Financial Services to send money back home.

Local attitudes toward the arrests abound with skepticism. One June 19 caller to a local talk show charged Ashcroft with targeting unstable Somali men to whip up fear and tension in the heartland. "I think that the Somalian community are just easy fodder for Mr. Ashcroft," he said. "They are black. That makes it very easy. They are powerless as well. I also think that it had something to do with Kerry's Columbus appearance Tuesday. It induces fear and panic reminding us of course that Bush is in control. It put Kerry's visit on the back burner."

Abdi and Faris might ultimately prove to be terrorists. But so far they seem just hapless patsies, their minds and spirits broken in a Bush-Ashcroft gulag more reminiscent of Stalin's Soviet Union and Saddam's Abu Ghraib than a nation governed by the rule of law.

The real source of terror here may be that this is precisely the kind of treatment in store for countless innocent Americans or foreign-born bystanders. The badge of terrorism can always be pinned on defenseless, marginalized people broken in the horrors of a prison system unconstrained by the Geneva Convention or the Bill of Rights.

Give Bush another four years, and it could happen to you.

June 20, 2004

FITRAKIS

Gott mit uns: On Bush and Hitler's rhetoric

President Bush told Texas evangelist James Robinson that "I feel like God wants me to run for President. I can't explain it, but I sense my country is going to need me. Something is going to happen . . . I know it won't be easy on me or my family, but God wants me to do it."

With 49.3% of New York City residents in a recent Zogby poll believing that some people in our government knew of the 911 attack in advance and allowed it to happen, the President as right-wing evangelical prophet is under siege in his Madison Square Garden bunker. Convention watchers should take careful note of the theocratic nationalist rhetoric at the Republican convention this week.

When was the last time a Western nation had a leader so obsessed with God and claiming God was on our side?

If you answered Adolph Hitler and Nazi Germany, you're correct. Nothing can be more misleading than to categorize Hitler as a barbaric pagan or Godless totalitarian, like Stalin.

Both Bush and Hitler believe that they were chosen by God to lead their nations. With Hitler boldly proclaiming, before launching his doctrine of preventive war against all of Europe, that

"I would like to thank Providence and the Almighty for choosing me of all people to be allowed to wage this battle for Germany."

"I follow the path assigned to me by Providence with the instinctive sureness of a sleepwalker," Hitler said.

Hitler stated in February 1940, "But there is something else I believe, and that is that there is a God. . . . And this God again has blessed our efforts during the past 13 years." After the Iraqi invasion, Bush announced, "God told me to strike at al Qaeda and I struck them, and then he instructed me to strike at Saddam, which I did . . . ." Neither the similarity between Hitler and Bush's religious rhetoric nor the fact that the current President's grandfather was called "Hitler's Angel" by the New York Tribune for his financing of the Fuher's rise to power is lost on Europeans.

Pat Robertson called Bush "a prophet" and Ralph Reed claimed, after the 9/11 attack, God picked the President because "he knew George Bush had the ability to lead in this compelling way." Hitler told the German people in March 1936, "Providence withdrew its protection and our people fell, fell as scarcely any other people heretofore. In this deep misery we again learn to pray. . . . The mercy of the Lord slowly returns to us again. And in this hour we sink to our knees and beseech our almighty God that he may bless us, that He may give us the strength to carry on the struggle for the freedom, the future, the honor, and the peace of our people. So help us God."

At the beginning of Hitler's crusade on April 12, 1922, he spelled out his version of the warmongering Jesus: "My feeling as a Christian points me to my Lord and Savior as a fighter." Randall Balmer in The Nation, noted that "Bush's God is the eye-for-an-eye God of the Hebrew prophets and the Book of Revelation, the God of vengeance and retribution."

As Bush has invoked the cross of Jesus to simultaneously attack the Islamic and Arab world, Hitler also saw the value of exalting the cross while waging endless war: "To be sure, our Christian Cross should be the most exalted symbol of the struggle against the Jewish-Marxist-Bolshevik spirit."

Like Bush-ites, Hitler was fond of invoking the Ten

Commandments as the foundation of Nazi Germany: "The Ten Commandments are a code of living to which there's no refutation. These precepts correspond to irrefragable needs of the human soul."

But if you ever wondered where Bush got his idea for so-called "faith-based initiatives" you need only consult Hitler's January 30, 1939 speech to the Reichstag. The Fuhrer begins, "Amongst the accusations which are directed against Germany in the so-called democracy is the charge that the National Socialist State is hostile to religion."

Hitler goes on to document how much "public monies derived from taxation through the organs of the State have been placed at the disposal of both churches [Protestant and Catholic]." Hitler gave nearly 1.8 billion Reichsmarks between 1933-1938 directly to the Christian churches. In 1938 alone, he bragged that the Nazis gave half a billion Reichsmarks from the national government and an additional 92 million Reichsmarks from the Nazi-controlled German states and parish associations.

Hitler made the intent of his faith-based initiative clear when he noted, "With a tenth of our budget for religion, we would thus have a Church devoted to the State and of unshakable loyalty. . . . the little sects, which receive only a few hundred thousand marks, are devoted to us body and soul."

Bush's assertion that "I trust God speaks through me. Without that, I couldn't do my job" brings to mind God as a dull-witted, cognitively-impaired nationalist unable to utter a simple declarative sentence who spends his time preaching "blessed are the warmongers and profit-makers."

September 1, 2004

WASSERMAN

Was Willie Horton Gay? Will George W. Bush be the hate-homosexuals candidate?

Few Americans now remember that George W. Bush's father was elected president in 1988 in one of the most racist campaigns ever staged in the United States. Now W. seems poised to follow in those tainted footsteps.

But the "issue" this time won't be race, it'll be gay marriage.

Early in the 1988 campaign, then-Vice President George H.W. Bush trailed then-Massachusetts Governor Michael Dukakis by as much as 15 points in the mainstream polls. Bush was sunk in a scandal-ridden Reagan Administration whose trademark was Iran Contra, the bizarre scam in which the Reaganites had illegally sold arms to Iranian fanatics and slipped the profits to right-wing contra rebels trying to overthrow the duly elected Sandinista government of Nicaragua. Reagan also sold chemical and biological weapons of mass destruction to Iraqi dictator, Saddam Hussein. Reagan's envoy to Saddam was now-Secretary of Defense Donald Rumsfeld.

Reagan was always more popular with the media than with the general public. Constantly proclaiming support for a balanced budget amendment, Reagan left the largest deficits in US history (until the coming of George W. Bush).

Bush One's run against Dukakis was hampered by his aloof, upper-crust lack of charisma. Runningmate Sen. Dan Quayle of Indiana was noted mainly for his deer-in-headlights demeanor. In a crucial televised debate, Quayle was utterly demolished by Dukakis's running mate, Texas Senator Lloyd Bentson.

But the Bush-Quayle team had a trump card---racism. Lee Atwater, the Karl Rove of the day, was a hard-driving, below-the-belt dirty trickster. Atwater seized on Willie Horton, a black prisoner who'd been paroled from the Massachusetts penal system and then committed another crime.

Atwater filled the air waves with brutally racist black-and-white ads meant to make Horton and Dukakis seem blood-related. The poisonous stench helped send the Democrats into a tail spin. Atwater later developed a brain tumor, and repented what he had done.

Karl Rove may soon step into Atwater's shoes. Recent decisions by the Supreme Courts of the US and Massachusetts against anti-sodomy laws have thrown the Christian Coalition and its national network of right-wing churches into a self-righteous tizzy.

For Rove, gay marriage is the new Willie Horton, a wedge issue perfectly suited to fire up the corporate-funded right-wing church network while diverting public attention from an ailing economy and a failing war effort.

Ironically, Vice President Dick Cheney's daughter is a lesbian whose personal right he has defended. As documented in David Brock's BLINDED BY THE RIGHT, the GOP has been continually lit up by closeted gays sickened by its vicious homophobia.

Rove, in turn, has not hesitated to attack Brock and anyone else opposing the Republican juggernaut. Bush has already let it be known he's inclined to support a Constitutional amendment banning gay marriage, and the Foxist media is starting to treat it as a major issue.

As governor of Vermont, Howard Dean approved gay civil unions, somewhat different from gay marriage. But the Bush/Rove GOP is unlikely to make such fine distinctions, any more than Bush One belabored the legal intricacies of the Willie Horton parole. Nor will they refrain from smearing other Democrats, whatever their actual stance, with the nastiest possible slant on gay rights.

What Papa Bush and Lee Atwater did to promote racism in American presidential campaigns, George W. and Karl Rove are poised to do for homophobia.

December 23, 2003

WASSERMAN

Was Bush's turkey trip to Baghdad aimed at Hillary Clinton?

The embedded corporate media is still crowing over the details of George W. Bush's Thanksgiving flight to Baghdad. The Shrub spinmeisters have branded it a "home run."

But the global image of the smirking Texan carrying that turkey on a tray will now join the "greatest hits" album headlined by Bush's "Mission Accomplished" shot on the USS Lincoln, since which more than 100 US soldiers have died.

The Fox media annointed to accompany Bush to Baghdad were barred from any uncontrolled interviews with American soldiers.

Historically, Bush was merely replaying Lyndon Johnson's tragic 1966 visit to Vietnam's Cam Ranh Bay, after which tens of thousands of American and Vietnamese soldiers and civilians died in nine years of ghastly slaughter.

Johnson swooped into the huge US with top secrecy and security. The saturation photo op was meant to boost Johnson's plummeting polls. Having won in 1964 as a peace candidate, LBJ's 1965 decision to escalate the war in Vietnam remains a catastrophic pivot point in US history.

At about two and a half hours, Johnson's stay at Cam Ranh Bay matched Bush's in Baghdad. LBJ visited none of Vietnam outside the base. The photo op gave him a fleeting lift amidst a relentless decline toward nervous collapse. Elected by one of the widest margins in US history, he shocked the world by declining to run for re-election, abandoning office in failure and disgrace.

Bush's re-run to Baghdad coincided with the death of yet another US soldier. More than sixty Americans were killed in November, the war's bloodiest month since Bush declared "Mission Accomplished." Overall more than 430 Americans have died in Iraq, with more than 2400 US wounded and thousands more Iraqis dead or maimed.

Like LBJ, Bush kept to military turf, and told the media he was prepared to abort the mission and flee toward home at any time. While there were no uncontrolled exchanges with US soldiers, Bush did meet briefly under top security with hand-picked Iraqis meant to serve in the American-engineered government to which Bush says he'll cede power next June, in the lead-up to the fall 2004 US elections.

But the extreme secrecy and nervous nature of the media stunt underscored that Iraqis are not "dancing in the streets" over the US occupation, as the Administration had originally promised when they were selling the American public on this war. Even members of the Governing Council weren't told of Bush's visit until they were brought to him. "We cannot consider Bush's arrival at Baghdad International Airport yesterday as a visit to Iraq," said Mahmoud Othman, a US-appointed member of Governing Council. "He did not meet with ordinary Iraqis. Bush was only trying to boost the morale of his troops."

A series of lethal anti-occupation attacks quickly followed, including a large ambush whose death toll is in dispute. US military officials now concede the Iraqi attacks are becoming better coordinated and more deadly.

Bush's Turkey Trot may have been aimed in part at upstaging New York Senator Hillary Rodham Clinton, who arrived in Baghdad the next day. Clinton and Rhode Island Senator Jack

Reed visited Afghanistan before coming to Baghdad. "I wanted to come to Iraq to let the troops know about the great job they're doing," said the former First Lady.

Clinton voted for the Congressional resolution used by the Administration to attack Iraq. She now says she is "a big believer that we ought to internationalize this" and bring in the United Nations. But that "will take a big change in our administration's thinking" and "I don't see that it's forthcoming."

Reed voted against the war's authorization. He says his November visit---he also came in June---re-confirmed his opposition. United Nations weapons inspectors should have been given more time to disarm Iraq, he says. Reed still questions the alleged links between Saddam Hussein and the September 11 terrorist attacks on New York.

An independent delegation of relatives and friends of US soldiers serving in Iraq and Afghanistan is scheduled to visit Baghdad soon. They plan to speak to grassroots Iraqis and to interview American soldiers unsupervised by US officials or embedded Foxoids.

Could this prompt another desperate, deadly Bush media distraction? Lyndon Johnson also used his Cam Ranh Bay visit to push reports of American deaths and domestic anti-war demonstrations off the front pages.

But given what followed, he---and our troops---should have stayed home. Shrub, take note.

December 2, 2003

WASSERMAN

What? No terror alert to herald the Osama Surprise?

Surprise! Surprise!! There have been no official terror alerts to interfere with the much-hyped Bush Bounce following last week's Republican National Convention.

And after waiting through the Labor Day weekend, with trial balloons floating about the long-awaited Osama Surprise, it's easy to see why.

Homeland Security Chief Tom Ridge has issued two terror alerts during the presidential campaign. One immediately followed John Kerry's choice of John Edwards as his running mate. The other immediately followed the Democratic National Convention.

The timing could not have been more obvious. Edwards' nomination generated a huge buzz for the Democrats. But the major media instantly turned to the intricacies of Ridge's bizarre, apocalyptic scare scam.

Then came a successful DNC. Again Ridge instantly screamed out breathless tales of a terrorist wolf, while the media slobbered at the door.

Ridge had only stale snippets, with no solid evidence for an imminent attack. There was no attack, and no arrests.

But both times, he negated crucial Democratic momentum. Fox

and its cohorts made the lack of a Kerry bounce the one-note theme of their post-convention coverage--while never mentioning the Ridge rants. Mission Accomplished.

In fact, the weeks of the Edwards nomination and DNC were calm by global standards.

But actual terrorism defined the week of the Republican National Convention. Two Russian passenger liners crashed with only one obvious explanation. Then terrorists staged a horrific Russian hostage crisis, leaving at least 300 dead.

Meanwhile, a half-million protestors swarmed into New York. Yet the only terror alert came from the Mayor's office on behalf of the grass in Central Park. Ridge's stark silence was a backhanded confirmation that the American peace movement can be counted on to remain non-violent, even in the face of its most vicious opponent.

It also underscored the double-standard that has made this administration so deeply loathed. With no credible evidence, but for obvious political gain, the Department of Homeland Security twice played cynical games with public terror alerts at the expense of the Democrats.

But with passenger planes being blown out of the sky, hundreds of Russian children held hostage and hordes of protestors descending on New York, nothing could be allowed to disrupt media coverage of the Republicans' Hate Show.

Ridge gave the GOP had an alert-free Labor Day weekend to crow about the post-convention bounce that might have been Kerry's. Team Rove also floated its first notice of an election-timed "capture" of Osama bin Laden. As millions have predicted, after three years the Administration may have miraculously "tracked him down" just in time for the November vote.

So will the next Homeland hyperventilation come when there's an actual threat to the public safety? Or will it happen to coincide with, say, a presidential debate? A Kerry/Edwards bounce? Or a Bush faux pas?

We are all pink with curiosity.

September 7, 2004

WASSERMAN & FITRAKIS

Kerry, Nader and the Greens need to kill the circular firing squad

It's time for the Kerry, Nader and Green campaigns to get locked in a room until they disarm the circular firing squad and focus on the real enemy, George W. Bush.

Especially in swing states like ours, the endless wrangling and rancor must stop. Every boring, suicidal attack harms our ability to beat Bush.

In light of his votes for war in Iraq, the Patriot Act and way too much else, it's obvious President Kerry will be no messiah. But we doubt our democracy or our planet would survive four more years of Cheney-Rove-Bush.

So we may ask friends in safe states like Massachusetts and Hawaii to balance our Kerry votes here in Ohio with votes there for Ralph or for the Green Party candidate, David Cobb.

If Al Gore had met and worked with Nader in 2000 instead of attacking him, we might have been spared the horrors of these past four years. It's inaccurate, unwise and self-destructive to continually blame Ralph for the Democrats' "loss" when in fact Gore won the election. We are glad Kerry has had the good sense to meet with Ralph, and to refrain from attacking the Greens.

But the three camps need to make a pro-active peace. Now!

Pat Buchanan clearly cost Bush some key states in 2000. The Republicans haven't spent the past four years screaming at him. But they did find a way to keep him from running in 2004.

Ralph has every right to run for president. Fighting to keep him off the ballot presumes the way to save democracy is to suppress it. It also presumes those who ultimately choose to vote for him are some sort of inanimate stolen property, wrongfully taken from the Democrats if only Ralph hadn't somehow brainwashed them into voting for him.

Please!!!

You can regret voting for   Nader in 2000. But he was not responsible for the Democrats' miserable campaign. Among other things, Nader should have been included in the presidential debates. Instead he was physically ejected from the first Gore-Bush debate, which Gore proceeded to lose.

The Democrats won the popular vote by 500,000 votes, but sat on their hands and kept their mouths wide shut while the Republicans stole the presidency. Gore's catastrophic mis-handling of the Florida debacle and his silence after it were catastrophic, and ran directly counter to the kinds of campaigns Nader has run---successfully---since 1963.

From the Liberty and Free Soil Parties through Lincoln's Republicans, the Greenbackers, Populists, Socialists, Progressives, Dixiecrats, Peace and Freedom Parties, Peronista/Reform Party, and Buchananites, third parties have been part of American presidential campaigns more often than not. Those who have accommodated and co-opted them rather than attacking them have been the ones to win the White House. Gore's polls ran consistently higher when he adopted the pro-peace, environmental and social justice stands Nader and the Greens have demanded. Rather than attacking Nader now, Kerry's Democrats should be adopting Green positions.

Nader ran in 1996, and in again in 2000. There is no mystery about what he or the Greens stand for. There's no excuse for anybody---Nader, the Greens or the Democrats---to attack each other in 2004.

We need a joint declaration of strategy from these three campaigns. We don't need Karl Rove smirking at yet another mass leftist suicide.

Franklin Roosevelt, against whom the Socialist Norman Thomas ran four times, honored him in the Oval Office for being the principled gentleman he was. FDR's victories were based in part on his co-option of key parts of the Socialist platforms, which Thomas graciously welcomed.

It's a time-honored model. Kerry, Nader and the Greens could all win if they follow it. It's unlikely democracy or our planet will survive if they don't.

August 15, 2004

COMPULSORY PATRIOTISM

Homey comes home: Bush in Columbus

The Nationwide Arena doors opened at 1:00. There would be a four-hour wait before the prodigal son returned to his ancestral home, Columbus, Ohio.

Forget about Kennebunkport, Maine. That's where George Herbert Walker of the St. Louis Walkers purchased a faux ancestral home. Ignore Connecticut. That's simply where Prescott Bush went, after his prank letter on being a war hero was published in a hometown newspaper embarrassing the family out of the heartland. Here in Columbus is where it all started. Where the great-grandfather of our current President began the family's well-documented tradition of war profiteering.

Samuel Bush, friend of the Rockefellers and owner of Buckeye Steel Castings, pulled his own "Halliburton" in World War I simultaneously serving on the Armaments Board and granting contracts to his family business. St. Paul's Episcopal Church still stands on Broad Street near downtown as a monument to the good old days. The Bush family worshipped there before its new generations embraced evangelical right-wing Christianity.

Karl Rove and the choreographers knew how to set the stage for the main event. There was former Buckeye linebacker great Chris Spielman muttering about the country needing more "church in the state, not more state in the church." Columbus has always been the kind of town that has seen the divinity in a brutal bone-crushing football player. Remember that game against Michigan? Clearly, he was filled with the Holy Spirit.

There was Ohio's most famous non-entity Mike DeWine babbling about the evil French, Germans and United Nations. It doesn't ever seem to occur to the Bush-ites that the United Nations and universal human rights were actually American ideas. You know, back in the Dark Ages when every President from FDR to Richard Nixon called themselves a "liberal." Granted, Nixon used the term "pragmatic liberal."

Nationwide, in a pattern developed over the past decade, transformed from a farmer's mutual insurance company to a for-profit "we love the GOP" carnivore, tried to keep protesters off the sidewalks surrounding the arena. An arena of course built with tax abatements, tax increment financing and other healthy infusions of public dollars for infrastructure. Nationwide and Bush agreed in principle on the joys of "wealthfare uber alles."

I stood outside with the two hundred demonstrators watching Bush on the giant video screen. Rove ingeniously tried to drive us off by arranging to play a rock video of Bush's bus tour snaking its way across the nation to New York City. The opening tune was Bachman Turner Overdrive's "Takin' Care of Business." Rather fitting. As I sang along I tried to inject the word "Big" before "Business" because Dubya surely has been working overtime making the world safe for plutocracy.

A key to the GOP strategy to win the Buckeye State is to put a Constitutional Amendment on the ballot banning gay marriage in Ohio. The Bush-ites perceive this wedge issue as essential bait to troll for the born-agains. I tried to think about the issue positively. After all, the only African Americans at the Bush rally, other than the token Clear Channel talk show host, were the paid canvassers trying to get the Bush people to sign the petition – some kind of wedge! Many Bush loyalists gladly lined up to sign in the shadow of Bush protesters with signs reading "Bush + Dick = Fucked."

Members of one group of half a dozen anti-Bush-ites were dressed like Bush with devil horns. They even had a cardboard cut-out of Bush with devil horns, prompting more than one Republican family to pose in front of it.

While devil horns seemed not to offend them, the one that said "Three Purple Hearts trumps Two DUIs" was denounced by Bush devotees as "tacky."

In keeping with the sports theme, Jack Nicklaus the Golden Bear, so-called because of the bundles of gold he's collected developing segregated upper-crust whitebread golf communities like Muirfield, introduced the President amidst cried of "four more years!" As the jocks took the edge off Bush's extremism, the President bounded on stage in a tan safari shirt doing that creepy little Hitler salute that he's now famous for. For a moment I thought the clever Rove had decided to dress the President so he'd look like Jack Hanna.

The demonstrators outside chanted, "This is what hypocrisy looks like!" One held up a sign that simply said "Hitler: Fatherland, Stalin: Motherland, Bush: Homeland." As I glanced quickly back at the screen, I swear I could see Jack Nicklaus and the faithful mouthing the words "Thousand Jahre Reich!"

The President led off by pointing out "My grandfather was raised here in Columbus, Ohio" and he asked his devotees, or is that deviltees, to send "a homeboy" back to the White House.

The old adage of it sounding better in the original German suddenly made sense.

The President described Dick Cheney as a "solid citizen," although he failed to point out of which Reich. In short order, the President promised that he would continue to heal the sick, raise the dead, make healthcare affordable, end frivolous lawsuits and allow untrained people to speculate in the stock market with their Social Security.

The demonstrators were now chanting "Ohio says no! Bush must go!" But inside, they were having their Nuremberg moment as Bush repeated his biggest and bestest lie – that Saddam had used weapons of mass destruction. I've always been impressed by this lie, and how they accomplish it. First, they take biochemical weapons given to Saddam by Ronald Reagan and George Bush the Elder and then these illegal limited war theater weapons are morphed into WMDs. Of course in reality, they're not. But in his fantasy world, the threats come from a broken and battered Iraqi nation with its $1.4 billion defense spending versus our $400 billion defense budget. We ignore the fact that some element of the Bush military industrial complex actually launched an anthrax attack on the U.S. media and the Democratic Party, which has gone unsolved.

Bush concluded: "Freedom is the almighty God's gift to every man and woman in the world." Sources tell me that the phrase struck out of the President's speech was the obvious next line: "Death mach frei."

On the way out, the mesmerized Nurembergers lined up and purchased "Gott mit uns" belt buckles and WWFD (What Would The Führer Do) bracelets from the giddy vendors.

September 1, 2004

THE KERRY BANDWAGON

WASSERMAN

The states of Iowa and the union agree: Bush can be beaten

Is the tide turning?

George W. Bush and his   puppetmaster Karl Rove tried to upstage the Democrats with a State of the Union Address full of tricks and gimmicks, Martian distractions and rattling sabers.

It backfired. The stunning results from Iowa far overshadowed Bush's lame, malapropic stump speech.   Space travel, gay marriage, steroids in baseball, these are the burning issues for a Republican Party smug enough to be certain they can steal any election.

The week's signature GOP moment came from Tom   DeLay's Texas, where a woman who sells vibrators was arrested for possessing more than two. In a state that's just been redistricted to prevent any Democrats from going to Congress, we see the GOP as the ultimate Luddites. Are Texas men that insecure? What will they ban next? Massage oil?

Come November, we can expect   Osama bin Laden to be miraculously "found" whenever Rove decides the timing is best.

A terrorist attack will explode here or there precisely as the Democrats gather steam. Bush may dump Dick Cheney into a cardiac unit to grab headlines and expand his base.

Remember, please, that Karl Rove, who runs the Bush apparatus, cut his teeth as a "Dirty Trickster" for Richard Nixon. Bush's father was elected in 1988 in the infamous "Willie Horton" campaign, the most racist in modern history.

These amoral assassins will fling the lowest available dirt on whoever got in their way, and nobody has mastered the craft better than Rove. With unlimited money to spend, your worst ethical nightmare is their bottom line.

But we're seeing a pattern here. Every time Bush jumps in the polls, he slumps back down.

From the gigantic rush he got after his " trifecta" on September 11, the polls fell to where they were before the terrorist attacks. From his "Mission Accomplished" flashdance on the decks of the Abraham Lincoln, back down he crashed as the bloodshed continued. From the "miraculous" capture of Saddam Hussein (where is he now?) the polls again plunged as the grassroots Iraqi resistance goes on. From the "booming" economy we see the Bush bounce going flat as no jobs materialize and deficits soar while the dollar slumps.

In short, George W. Bush is still George W. Bush: ruthless, corrupt, untrustworthy, closed-minded, authoritarian, inarticulate, intellectually challenged, programmed, cynical, dishonest, violent, a draft dodger and a religious fanatic who believes he speaks to and for God.

Through the Christian Coalition the GOP has a solid activist base of fanatic puritan fundamentalists unparalleled in US history. They have unlimited money. And they have control of the mainstream media, whose endless gush of right-wing bloviaters has just one mantra: "Bush will win, Bush will win, Bush will win."

But they can be beaten. Here are some of the things that must happen:

1) THE VOTES MUST BE HONESTLY COUNTED: As push comes to shove, there is only one issue in this campaign: will the votes be honestly counted. As Stalin infamously put it: it doesn't matter who casts them, only who counts them. We know that the 2000 election was stolen, and that the GOP would be more than happy to do it again through rigged voting machines without paper trails, the computerized disenfranchisement of "convicted

felons" and other suspected Democrats, and whatever else Rove & company can come up with.

2) THE VOTES MUST BE HONESTLY COUNTED: In 2000 Al Gore sat passively and watched as the White House was stolen. This time, all serious candidates must hammer at this issue, over and over. Rep. Rush Holt's bill now in Congress to require a paper trail for computerized voting machines is just a start, but it's a good one. The Democrats must get that passed or let the nation know why it didn't, and what that really means if the GOP claims victory in November.

3) THE VOTES MUST BE HONESTLY COUNTED: But it won't be enough just to raise the issue. In every state there must be campaign committees explicitly charged with fighting the pre-election disenfranchisements that happened in Florida and elsewhere. There must be extensive inspection of all voting machines, ballots and other election procedures. The polls must be monitored. Unless the Democrats take concrete, effective steps to guarantee a fair vote count, there's no reason to bother with this election at all.

4-10) THE VOTES MUST BE HONESTLY COUNTED: It may also not be sufficient for the Democrats alone to do this. Serious petitioning must now be done to the United Nations, the government of Switzerland or whoever else might serve as a honest broker, willing to serve an international watch dog function to help guarantee the coup that began in 2000 is not given four more years to solidify power.

11) THE HOUSE MUST BE RE-REDISTRICTED: Through redistricting the GOP has already guaranteed that the Democrats have virtually no chance of ever re-taking the House of Representatives. In one fell swoop, with typical vicious cynicism, Rove and DeLay have eliminated a dozen Texas Democrats even before the election is held. Nationwide, the system is now so twisted Democrats could carry the composite House vote by a wide margin and still end up vastly outnumbered on the floor. This was not the intent of the nation's Founders and must be changed, by Constitutional Amendment if necessary. Millions of us, especially

in urban areas, have been effectively disenfranchised for years. The Democrats must publicize this curse on the Congress, and then do something about it.

12) PREPARE FOR RACISM & HOMOPHOBIA---The stench from George H.W. Bush's racist 1988 Willie Horton campaign still taints the presidency. In 2000 the GOP machine specifically targeted African-American and Jewish voters in Florida, Tennessee, Arkansas and elsewhere with Jim Crow tactics that threw those states---and the election---to Bush. This year we can expect similar racism and the smearing of gays and whoever else might be available to mobilize the extremist "religious" right. Somebody should replay those Willie Horton ads to remind the nation who these people really are.

13) ENOUGH ABOUT RALPH NADER, ALREADY: For four years Democrats have indulged in blaming Ralph Nader and the Greens for "losing" the 2000 election. But Al Gore won by 500,000 votes. Add Nader's 2.7 million and 2000 represented a powerful Dem-green mandate, which Bush aborted. THAT'S what the Dems should have been screaming about for the past four years.

14) BUSH-ROVE WERE GOING TO STEAL THE ELECTION NO MATTER WHAT: Nader's supporters were not the mindless property of the Democratic party that Ralph somehow hijacked. And a GOP capable of stealing 16,000 votes in a single Florida district was more than capable of stealing all they needed, Nader or no.

15) PICK UP THE PHONE: Nader remains the most effective citizen activist in recent US history. He still draws huge (paying) crowds. He has a phone. And an office with a door that opens. So do the activists who chose to support him, and may yet again if the Dems repeat their folly of 2000. A few phone calls, some meaningful conversation, a search for common ground, some POLITICS, and maybe the Dems can mobilize at least part of an activist hard core they absurdly blew off in 2000. There's absolutely no excuse for doing otherwise.

16) FORGET THE CONFEDERACY: Conversely, those folks

driving around with Confederate flags are going to vote for Bush. The old Slave South (Bush's REAL taproot) is not going to come around. But as Norman Solomon and others have pointed out, the Hispanic southwest (Arizona, New Mexico, Colorado) is in reach and needs to be worked on. If, by miracle, Florida or Texas can be got, it's with Hispanic, not racist white votes. How about New Mexico's Hispanic Gov. Bill Richardson for VP?

17) REMEMBER THE ENVIRONMENT: Not even the bought corporate media can hide that Bush has launched a total kamikaze assault on the natural planet. This is an issue the resonates even with much of the fundamentalist right. Mother Earth is still right up there with apple pie. Forget the Confederate flag. Wave the Green one!!!!!

18) REPEAL THE PATRIOT ACT: Bush's one legitimate applause line was that the Patriot Act is about to expire. Even right wingers like William Safire have been lining up against it. The Dems startled poor Georgie when they clapped for that line in his otherwise pathetic State of the Union. Much of the nation, left and right, feels the same. Use it!

19) REMEMBER WATERGATE AND VALERIE PLAME: Somebody very high up in the White House, probably Karl Rove and/or Dick Cheney, has committed a serious felony (and pissed off the CIA) by outing covert operative Valerie Plame. This cancer is eating away at the junta's core. If there is a single issue to push push push alongside the economy, that may be it. Think dagger to the Constitution. Think Dick Nixon, August 9, 1974, getting on that Plame...er, plane.

20) YOU GOTTA BELIEVE: The mainstream mantra that Bush can't be beaten is only true if we let them steal the vote count again. They've got the money. But they've got Bush. The "inevitability" of his victory is as deep as the headlights in his deer.

21) THE HARDER THEY COME: Our theme song. Buy the Jimmy Cliff album. Dance the dance. "...as sure as the sun will shine.......the harder they come, the harder they fall, one and all....."
January 22, 2004

FITRAKIS

E-Voting: The new battle hymn of the republic

The fight for Ohio's 20 electoral votes this November is being waged in the courts, the election boards, the polling places and the streets.

When Secretary of State J. Kenneth Blackwell halted the purchase of new electronic voting machines on July 16 after two investigations identified 57 potential software and hardware security threats, North Canton, Ohio's Diebold Electronic Systems' dream of a $100 million contract with the state disappeared.

And so may have Diebold CEO "Wally" O'Dell's promise to "deliver" the Buckeye State's electoral votes, and the presidency, to George W. Bush in Ohio. As we keep hearing in the press, no Republican candidate has ever won the presidency without Ohio's electoral votes.

Still, the fear of the dreaded   DREs (Direct Record Electronic) machines has produced political and legal skirmishes throughout this key battleground state. The Electronic Frontier Foundation, the Verified Voting Foundation, VotersUnite! and Citizens Alliance for Secure Elections (CASE) filed an *Amicus Curiae* brief in the U.S. District Court for the Northern District of Ohio in late July.

The brief was in response to a lawsuit filed by the National Federation of the Blind (NFB) to force 31 counties to adopt electronic voting machines that are arguably more accessible for sight-impaired voters. Oddly, the Federation has emerged not only as an advocate for the blind, but as a staunch advocate of Diebold. When the *Free Press* contacted the Ohio Federation for the Blind President Barbara Pierce for comment regarding their avid support for Diebold, she said the Diebold machines "are the most robust." When pressed for details, she could not supply any specifics on the particular nature of Diebold's robustness.

The *Free Press* tested five electronic voting machines on display at the State Capitol and found the machines virtually indistinguishable except for the fact that two provided a verifiable paper audit trail and the others, including Diebold, did not.

When asked whether or not a million-dollar grant from Diebold toward the construction of the Federation's National Research and Training Institute for the Blind had influenced her organization's opinion, Pierce replied, "Absolutely not, the issues are completely separate."

In a November 1, 2000 press release entitled "Diebold and NFB partner to develop next generation voice-G ATMs," O'Dell said, "NFB has long been actively involved in promoting adaptive technologies which allow the blind to live and work independently in today's technology-driven world." In that world, Diebold is one of the largest producers of ATMs. Curiously, all of Diebold's ATM machines provide paper receipts while its electronic "black box" voting machines do not.

Shortly after O'Dell's infamous August 14, 2003 letter to Central Ohio Republicans in which he stated that he is personally "committed to helping Ohio deliver its electoral votes to the President next year," he came under attack for his partisan politics. Suddenly, the beneficiaries of his largesse – various disability rights activists, most notably associated with the NFB – began to loudly champion Diebold's voting machines.

Following O'Dell's comments and a devastating report from computer science professors at Johns Hopkins University on the vulnerabilities of DREs, the American Association of People with Disabilities (AAPD) in a written statement dismissed critics of paperless voting machines as "a rising chorus of geeks." The AAPD claims that a paper trail would lead to vote buying and fraud. However, the paper trail machines observed by the *Free Press* all had designs which kept the audit paper trail under plexiglass then dropped it into a secured dropbox. There was no voting receipt given to the voter to show anyone wishing to purchase the vote.

The *Amicus* brief argues three key points: "A growing body of evidence demonstrates that the majority of electronic voting machines currently in use are not sufficiently secure"; that "there are a variety of available, tested technologies that can be used to allow accessible voting without compromising security"; and that "the emerging evidence suggests that currently available DREs are not yet the panacea for disabled voters that they have been advertised to be."

The brief documents 18 major documented voting fiascos linked to DRE technologies. The list includes, in part: Diebold touch screens that when pressed for one party, registered the vote for the other; software programming errors that left votes improperly tabulated; battery problems; votes failing to register on the screen; votes simply disappearing or not being recorded; X's dimming out and migrating to the other party; and machines that failed to operate.

Here in Central Ohio, DREs switched the vote in the 1998 election awarding votes to Democratic challenger Ed Brown instead of incumbent representative John Kasich. The vote, as originally tabulated by the electronic voting machines, registered 62.9% for Congressman Kasich. The corrected number, agreed to by Brown was 67.2%. Brown, a computer expert, said the problem was with the software and that it was easy to figure out that he wasn't beating Kasich "80 to 20 in the Republican stronghold of Westerville."

In 1992, votes in the inner city of Columbus were swapped in the Democratic primary with a rural candidate winning a core precinct of an urban Democrat.

There are already two DRE machines equipped with voter-verified paper ballots certified in Ohio. These are AccuPoll and Avante Vote-Tracker. Moreover, both Sequoia Voting Systems and TruVote were in the process of being certified with voter-verified paper trail machines when the brief was filed.

The brief urges the court not to allow any "voting machine technologies unless they contained a voter verified paper ballot."

"This can help ensure that voters have confidence that their votes are being counted as cast, that voters do not become disenfranchised due to malfunctions election day and, most importantly, that the individuals who get the most votes are actually elected. It is difficult to imagine a more important task this election year," the brief ends.

A political skirmish over electronic voting broke out after an intensive Computer-Ate-My-Vote campaign, culminating in rallies in 19 states including Ohio, where 20,000 votes opposing "black box voting" were delivered to Blackwell's office. After Howard Dean's Democracy for America group participated in the rallies, calling for electronic voting machines to produce paper receipts, Rep. Bob Nay of Ohio fired off a letter to Dean stating, "Left-wing groups like yours . . . that are exploiting this issue to inflame your supporters and raise money for yourselves are recklessly making claims that are unsupported by the facts."

Gov. Dean, on behalf of his dangerous "left-wing" group, had issued the following statement: "We cannot and must not put the success of one party or another above the good of our entire country and all our people. In a democracy, you always count the votes no matter who wins."

Two days later, Blackwell stopped the rush to black box voting in Ohio. Blackwell made his decision with Diebold under fire in California following a disastrous March primary where 573 of 1038 polling places failed to open on time due to computer malfunctions in San Diego County. In Alameda County, at least 6000 voters were forced to use paper ballots after Diebold machines failed. California's Attorney General Bill Lockyer officially decertified Diebold machines.

On July 9, Lockyer unsealed a whistle-blower's lawsuit against Diebold filed by Bev Harris, the author of *Black Box Voting* and computer programmer Jim March. The suit demanded that Diebold fully reimburse the state for the equipment purchases.

Critics of Diebold, like British investigative journalist Greg Palast, point out that "Canada and Sweden vote on paper ballot with little spoilage and without suspicious counts."

With black box voting beaten back, new fears are arising in the "swing state" of Ohio after revelations from Citizens for Legitimate Government that 105,000 voters have been purged for "inactivity" in Hamilton County. The purging of voter rolls in Greater Cincinnati, in the key battleground state, after the Florida voter purges and electoral debacle of 2000, may briefly shift the focus of groups like Citizens Alliance for Secure Elections away from electronic voting. In the 2000 election, the Florida Secretary of State's office, run by Bush's Florida campaign manager Kathleen Harris, failed to process some 600,000 newly registered voters and incorrectly disenfranchised 58,000 voters – over half of them black – because their names or date of birth were the same or similar to felons. The new battle in the Buckeye State, commonly referred to as "Ground Zero" in this Presidential election, will be to ensure that Florida's Jim Crow purges of black voters don't occur across the Mason-Dixon line.

September 3, 2004

"It's not who votes that counts. It's who counts the votes."

—apocryphally attributed to Iosef Vissarionovich Stalin, Soviet revolutionary, political leader, party animal and all-around scary character.

Diebold. Because democracy is too important to leave to chance.

DIEBOLD

We won't rest.

©2004 salamander.eps

FITRAKIS & WASSERMAN

Diebold's Political Machine

Political insiders suggest Ohio could become as decisive this year as Florida was four years ago. Which is why the state's plan to use paperless touch-screen voting machines has so many up in arms.

Soccer moms and NASCAR dads come and go, but swing states are always in fashion. And this year, Ohio is emerging as the most fashionable of the bunch. Asked recently about the importance of Ohio in this year's presidential campaign, one veteran of Buckeye State politics told *Salon*, "Ohio is the Florida of 2004."

That label sounds ominously accurate to the many who are skeptical of computerized voting. In addition to being as decisive as the 2000 polling in Florida, they worry this year's vote in Ohio could be just as flawed. Specifically, they worry that it could be rigged. And they wonder why state officials seem so unconcerned by the fact that the two companies in line to sell touch-screen voting machines to Ohio have deep and continuing ties to the Republican Party. Those companies, Ohio's own Diebold Election Systems and Election Systems & Software of Nebraska, are lobbying fiercely ahead of a public hearing on the matter in Columbus next week.

There's solid reason behind the political rhetoric tapping Ohio as a key battleground. No Republican has ever captured the White House without carrying Ohio, and only John Kennedy managed the feat for the Democrats. In 2000, George W. Bush won in the Buckeye State by a scant four percentage points. Four years earlier, Bill Clinton won in Ohio by a similar margin.

In recent years, central Ohio has been transformed from a bastion of Republicanism into a Democratic stronghold. Six of Columbus' seven city council members are Democrats, as is the city's mayor, Michael Coleman. But no Democrat has been elected to Congress from central Ohio in more than 20 years, and the area around Columbus still includes pockets where no Democrat stands a chance. One such Republican pocket is Upper Arlington, the Columbus suburb that is home to Walden "Wally" O'Dell, the chairman of the board and chief executive of Diebold. For years, O'Dell has given generously to Republican candidates. Last September, he held a packed $1,000-per-head GOP fundraiser at his 10,800-square-foot mansion. He has been feted as a guest at President Bush's Texas ranch, joining a cadre of "Pioneers and Rangers" who have pledged to raise more than $100,000 for the Bush reelection campaign. Most memorably, O'Dell last fall penned a letter pledging his commitment "to helping Ohio deliver its electoral votes to the President."

O'Dell has defended his actions, telling the Cleveland Plain Dealer "I'm not doing anything wrong or complicated." But he also promised to lower his political profile and "try to be more sensitive." But the Diebold boss' partisan cards are squarely on the table. And, when it comes to the Diebold board room, O'Dell is hardly alone in his generous support of the GOP. One of the longest-serving Diebold directors is W.R. "Tim" Timken. Like O'Dell, Timken is a Republican loyalist and a major contributor to GOP candidates. Since 1991 the Timken Company and members of the Timken family have contributed more than a million dollars to the Republican Party and to GOP presidential candidates such as George W. Bush. Between 2000 and 2002 alone, Timken's Canton-based bearing and steel company gave more than $350,000 to Republican causes, while Timken himself gave more than $120,000. This year, he is one of George W. Bush's campaign Pioneers, and has already pulled in more than $350,000 for the president's reelection bid.

While Diebold has received the most attention, it actually isn't the biggest maker of computerized election machines. That honor goes to Omaha-based ES&S, and its Republican roots may be even stronger than Diebold's.

The firm, which is privately held, began as a company called Data Mark, which was founded in the early 1980s by Bob and Todd Urosevich. In 1984, brothers William and Robert Ahmanson bought a 68 percent stake in Data Mark, and changed the company's name to American Information Services (AIS). Then, in 1987, McCarthy & Co, an Omaha investment group, acquired a minority share in AIS.

In 1992, investment banker Chuck   Hagel, president of McCarthy & Co, became chairman of AIS. Hagel, who had been touted as a possible Senate candidate in 1993, was again on the list of likely GOP contenders heading into the 1996 contest. In January of 1995, while still chairman of ES&S, Hagel told the Omaha *World-Herald* that he would likely make a decision by mid-March of 1995. On March 15, according to a letter provided by Hagel's Senate staff, he resigned from the AIS board, noting that he intended to announce his candidacy. A few days later, he did just that.

A little less than eight months after stepping down as director of AIS, Hagel surprised national pundits and defied early polls by defeating Benjamin Nelson, the state's popular former governor. It was Hagel's first try for public office. Nebraska elections officials told *The Hill* that machines made by AIS probably tallied 85 percent of the votes cast in the 1996 vote, although Nelson never drew attention to the connection. Hagel won again in 2002, by a far healthier margin. That vote is still angrily disputed by Hagel's Democratic opponent, Charlie Matulka, who did try to make Hagel's ties to ES&S an issue in the race and who asked that state elections officials conduct a hand recount of the vote. That request was rebuffed, because Hagel's margin of victory was so large.

As might be expected, Hagel has been generously supported by his investment partners at McCarthy & Co. -- since he first ran,

Hagel has received about $15,000 in campaign contributions from McCarthy & Co. executives. And Hagel still owns more than $1 million in stock in McCarthy & Co., which still owns a quarter of ES&S.

If the Republican ties at   Diebold and ES&S aren't enough to cause concern, argues election reform activist Bev Harris, the companies' past performances and current practices should be. Harris is author of Black Box Voting, and the woman behind the BlackBoxVoting.com web site.

The rush to embrace computerized voting, of course, began with Florida. But, in fact, one of the Sunshine State's election-day disasters was the direct result of a malfunctioning computerized voting system; a system built by Diebold. The massive screwup in Volusia County was all but lost in all the furor over hanging chads and butterfly ballots in South Florida. In part that's because county election officials avoided a total disaster by quickly conducting a hand recount of the more than 184,000 paper ballots used to feed the computerized system. But the huge computer miscount led several networks to incorrectly call the race for Bush.

The first signs that the Diebold-made system in Volusia County was malfunctioning came early on election night, when the central ballot-counting computer showed a Socialist Party candidate receiving more than 9,000 votes and Vice President Al Gore getting minus 19,000. Another 4,000 votes poured into the plus column for Bush that didn't belong there. Taken together, the massive swing seemed to indicate that Bush, not Gore, had won Florida and thus the White House. Election officials restarted the machine, and expressed confidence in the eventual results, which showed Gore beating Bush by 97,063 votes to 82,214. After the recount, Gore picked up 250 votes, while Bush picked up 154. But the erroneous numbers had already been sent to the media.

Harris has posted a series of internal Diebold memos relating to the Volusia County miscount on her website, BlacBboxVoting.com. One memo from Lana Hires of Global Election Systems, now part of Diebold, complains, "I need some answers! Our department is being audited by the County. I have been waiting for someone to give me an explanation as to why Precinct 216 gave Al Gore a minus 16,022 [votes] when it was uploaded." Another, from Talbot Ireland, Senior VP of Research and Development for Diebold, refers to key "replacement" votes in Volusia County as "unauthorized."

Harris has also posted a post-mortem by CBS detailing how the network managed to call Volusia County for Bush early in the morning. The report states: "Had it not been for these [computer] errors, the CBS News call for Bush at 2:17:52 AM would not have been made." As Harris notes, the 20,000-vote error shifted the momentum of the news reporting and nearly led Gore to concede.

What's particularly troubling, Harris says, is that the errors were caught only because an alert poll monitor noticed Gore's vote count going *down* through the evening, which of course is impossible. Diebold blamed the bizarre swing on a "faulty memory chip," which Harris claims is simply not credible. The whole episode, she contends, could easily have been consciously programmed by someone with a partisan agenda. Such claims might seem far-fetched, were it not for the fact that a cadre of computer scientists showed a year ago that the software running Diebold's new machines can be hacked with relative ease.

The hackers posted some 13,000 pages of internal documents on various web sites – documents that were pounced on by Harris and others. A desperate Diebold went to court to stop this "wholesale reproduction" of company material. By November of last year, the Associated Press reported that Diebold had sent cease-and-desist letters to programmers and students at two dozen universities, including the University of California at Berkeley and the Massachusetts Institute of Technology. The letters were ignored by at least one group of students at Swarthmore College, who vowed an "electronic civil disobedience" campaign.

Equally troubling, of course, is the fact that the touch-screen systems Diebold, ES&S, and the other companies have on the market now aren't designed to generate a polling place paper trail. While ES&S says it is open to providing voter receipts, and has even designed a prototype machine that does so, the company isn't going to roll that prototype into production until state and federal elections officials make it mandatory.

Lawmakers in Congress and the Ohio legislature are scrambling to do just that. In Ohio, State Sen. Teresa Fedor of Toledo has proposed a bill requiring a "voter verified paper audit trail" for all elections in the state. Congressman Rush Holt of New Jersey is pushing a similar measure in Washington. But the efforts are being fought by Republicans in both places. In Ohio, Secretary of State Kenneth Blackwell has already signed $100 million in agreements to purchase voting machines. The bulk of the purchases would go to Diebold and ES&S, and Blackwell insists there is no need for paper receipts. Considering the political opposition and the companies' wait-and-see approach, it's almost certain that voters using touch-screen machines in November will walk away from their polling places without ever seeing a printed record of their choices.

At a trade fair held recently here in Columbus, a wide range of companies seeking to fill that void demonstrated technologies that could easily and cheaply provide paper receipts for ballots. One such product, called TruVote, provides two separate voting receipts. The first is shown under plexiglass, and displays the choices made by a vote on the touch screen. This copy falls into a lockbox after the voter approves it. The second is provided to the voter. TruVote is already attracting fans, among them Brooks Thomas, Tennessee's Coordinator of Elections. "I've not seen anything that compares to [the] TruVote validation system." Georgia's Assistant Secretary of State, Terrell L. Slayton, Jr., calls the device is the "perfect solution." But Blackwell argues the campaign for a paper ballot trail for Ohio is an attempt to "derail" reform. He says he'll comply with the demand only if Congress mandates it.

Meanwhile, in Upper Arlington, a 'lower profile' Wally O'Dell and his wife recently petitioned the city to get permission to serve liquor at future fundraisers and political gatherings.

March 5, 2004

Bismarck was right.

At Diebold we cook the results.
So that you don't have to.

We won't rest.

©2004 salamander.eps

Artist's disclaimer: "This page and these images are no way no how affiliated with Diebold Inc., and the statements in the "ads" (let's call them parodies, which might let me off the hook for the appropriation of the Diebold name and chop under "fair use") are not necessarily representative of the opinions of Diebold's executives, shareholders or worker bees, no, not even in their dark malignant hearts, and did I mention that I hold the legal profession in the highest regard? Diebold is a registered trademark of Diebold Corporation. Any other marks are the property of their respective owners."

FITRAKIS

Death of a patriot

The subject line on yesterday's email read: "Another mysterious accident solves a Bush problem. Athan Gibbs dead, Diebold lives." The attached news story briefly described the untimely Friday, March 12th death of perhaps America's most influential advocate of a verified voting paper trail in the era of touch screen computer voting. Gibbs, an accountant for more than 30 years and the inventor of the TruVote system, died when his vehicle collided with an 18-wheeled truck which rolled his Chevy Blazer several times and forced it over the highway retaining wall where it came to rest on its roof.

Coincidence theorists will simply dismiss the death of Gibbs as a tragic accident – the same conclusion these coincidence theorists came to when anti-nuclear activist Karen Silkwood died in November 1974 when her car struck a concrete embankment en route to a meeting with New York Times reporter David Burnham. Prominent independent investigators concluded that Silkwood's car was hit from behind and forced off the road. Silkwood was reportedly carrying documents that would expose illegal activities at the Kerr-McGee nuclear fuel plant. The FBI report found that she fell asleep at the wheel after overdosing on Quaaludes and that there never were any such files. A journalist secretly employed by the FBI, and a veteran of the Bureau's COINTELPRO operation against political activists, provided testimony for the FBI report.

Gibbs' death bears heightened scrutiny because of the way he lived his life after the 2000 Florida election debacle. I interviewed

Athan Gibbs in January of this year. "I've been an accountant, an auditor, for more than thirty years. Electronic voting machines that don't supply a paper trail go against every principle of accounting and auditing that's being taught in American business schools," he insisted.

"These machines are set up to provide paper trails. No business in America would buy a machine that didn't provide a paper trail to audit and verify its transaction. Now, they want the people to purchase machines that you can't audit? It's absurd."

Gibbs was in Columbus, Ohio proudly displaying his TruVote machine that offered a "VVPAT, that's a voter verified paper audit trail" he noted.

Gibbs also suggested that I look into the "people behind the other machines." He offered that "Diebold and ES&S are real interesting and all Republicans. If you're an investigative reporter go ahead and investigate. You'll find some interesting material."

Gibbs' TruVote machine is a marvel. After voters touch the screen, a paper ballot prints out under plexiglass and once the voter compares it to his actual vote and approves it, the ballot drops into a lockbox and is issued a numbered receipt. The voter's receipt allows the track his particular vote to make sure that it was transferred from the polling place to the election tabulation center.

My encounter with Gibbs led to a cover story in the Columbus Free Press March-April issue, entitled, "Diebold, electronic voting and the vast right-wing conspiracy." The thesis I advanced in the Free Press article is that some of the same right-wing individuals who backed the CIA's covert actions and overthrowing of democratic elections in the Third World in the 1980s are now involved in privatized touch screen voting. Additionally I co-wrote an article with Harvey Wasserman that was posted at MotherJones.com on March 5, 2004. Both articles outlined ties between far right elements of the Republican Party and Diebold and ES&S, which count the majority of the nation's electronic votes.

As I wrote in the Free Press article, "Proponents of a paper trail were emboldened when Athan Gibbs, President and CEO of

TruVote International, demonstrated a voting machine at a vendor's fair in Columbus that provides two separate voting receipts."

In an interview on WVKO radio, Gibbs calmly and methodically explained the dangers of "black box" touch screen voting. "It absolutely makes no sense to buy electronic voting machines that can't produce a paper trail. Inevitably, computers mess up. How are you going to have a recount, or correct malfunctions without a paper trail?

Now, the man asking the obvious question, and demonstrating an obvious tangible solution is dead in another tragic accident, a week after both articles were in circulation.

When I called TruVote International to verify Gibbs' death, I reached Chief Financial Officer Adrenne Brandon who assured me "We're going on in his memory. We're going to make this happen."

Every American concerned with democracy should pledge to make this happen. To beat back the rush for state governments to purchase privatized, partisan and unreliable electronic voting machines without verified paper trails.

Gibbs' last words to me were "How do you explain what happened to Senator Max Cleland in Georgia. How do you explain that? The Maryland study and the Johns Hopkins scientists have warned us against 'blind faith voting.' These systems can be hacked into. They found patches in Georgia and the people servicing the machine had entered the machines during the voting process. How can we the people accept this? No more blind faith voting."

March 17, 2004

Diebold. Because it's the 21ˢᵗ century, for crying out loud.

Artist's disclaimer: "This page and these images are no way no how affiliated with Diebold Inc., and the statements in the "ads" (let's call them parodies, which might let me off the hook for the appropriation of the Diebold name and chop under "fair use") are not necessarily representative of the opinions of Diebold's executives, shareholders or worker bees, no, not even in their dark malignant hearts, and did I mention that I hold the legal profession in the highest regard? Diebold is a registered trademark of Diebold Corporation. Any other marks are the property of their respective owners."

FITRAKIS

The year democracy ended

As the year ends, 2003 will be remembered by future historians as the year the pretense of democracy in the United States ended.

Since the 1940s, conservatives have accepted the assumption of economist Joseph Schumpeter that democracy in a mass society existed of little more than the following: the adult population could vote; the votes were fairly counted; and the masses could choose between elites from one of two parties.

With the most recent revelations about the 2000 Bush coup in Florida disclosed in the shocking stolen Diebold memos, the Bush family has signaled that an authoritarian right-wing dynasty is the future course for American politics.

The Sunday, November 12, 2000 Washington Post, buried on page A22, the smoking gun of the Bush family's CIA-style rigged "demonstration" election in Florida: "Something very strange happened on election night to Deborah Tannenbaum, a Democratic Party official of Volusia County. At 10 p.m., she called the county elections department and found that Al Gore was leading George W. Bush 83,000 votes to 62,000 votes. But when she checked the county's Web site for an update half an hour later, she found a startling development: Gore's count had dropped by 16,000 votes, while an obscure Socialist candidate had picked up 10,000 ... all because of a single precinct with only 600 voters."

So it should come as no surprise when the New York Times headline on July 24 of this year read "Computer voting is open to easy fraud." The work by Alastair Thompson at scoop.co.nz and Bev Harris in her essential new book Black Box Voting reveal not only that computer voting is open to fraud but that massive and widespread fraud occurred in the 2000 election.

Moreover, the emboldened Bush administration appears to have continued its fraud in the 2002 and subsequent elections. Why not? The investigation by Senator Frank Church in the 1970s revealed that the U.S. CIA routinely rigged elections throughout the world and was involved in overthrowing democracies and installing dictatorships as needed during the Cold War. The list is familiar to human rights advocates: Iran and Guatemala in the 50s; Chile and Greece in the 70s.

Four computer scientists at Rice University and a separate study by the Security Institute at Johns Hopkins University document how easy it is to hack into the Diebold voting machines. Diebold's CEO Wally O'Dell is an ardent Bush supporter who recently hosted a $10,000-a-plate fundraiser for the President in his manor in the affluent Columbus suburb of Upper Arlington. He is "committed to helping Ohio deliver its electoral votes to the President next year" while, at the same time, attempting to contract with the state of Ohio for his fabulously flawed voting machines.

And it's not just Diebold. The largest seller of computerized voting systems in the U.S. is ES&S, whose former top exec is now Nebraska's Republican Senator Chuck Hagel, who won after ES&S machines reported an unusual and stunning black vote for him.

The Dallas News reported that early voting in the 2002 election created ". . . several dozen complaints . . . from people who said that they selected a Democratic candidate but that their vote appeared beside the name of a Republican on the screen."

Recall the six major upsets of Democrats by Republicans in Georgia in the 2002 election. The state's votes were counted on the unreliable and easily hackable 22,000 Diebold machines. Also during the 2002 election, where over 1000 votes were cast in other races, no votes were registered for governor as Clinton administration Attorney General went down to a surprisingly 5000 vote loss.

As a result of these obvious voting irregularities, hackers went into the Diebold system and stole thousands of documents and internal memos which expose the 2000 Florida coup. In Harris' book based on these documents and interviews with Diebold officials, she outlines how Gore originally conceded the election after somebody used a "second [computer] card (card #3) that mysteriously appeared, subtracted 16,022 from Al Gore and still in some undefined way, added 4000 erroneous votes to George W. Bush . . ."

A summary of the 2002 election by scoop.co.nz found that in 14 races, there was a 3-16 point swing to the Republican Party after the final poll was taken providing several stunning upsets. By contrast, in only two races was there a swing toward the Democratic Party, between 2-4 points. In three other races, the pollsters were within the margin of error.

The American people have been socialized into denial. First about the ruthless and imperialist nature of their 26 intelligence-gathering agencies including the CIA and NSA that have been involved in rigging elections worldwide and the ongoing involvement by these agencies in American politics. What is obviously evolved is a praetorian guard, loyal only to the Bush family, that some call the "shadow government."

Most Americans are intent to stick their heads in the sand on Bush's vote-rigging and our troops in the sands of Iraq. Future historians will record that while the facts and documentation of the end of American republic mounted, many believed the babbling of a low-IQ'ed well-scripted son of the new aristocracy.

November 30, 2003

Artist's disclaimer: "This page and these images are no way no how affiliated with Diebold Inc., and the statements in the "ads" (let's call them parodies, which might let me off the hook for the appropriation of the Diebold name and chop under "fair use") are not necessarily representative of the opinions of Diebold's executives, shareholders or worker bees, no, not even in their dark malignant hearts, and did I mention that I hold the legal profession in the highest regard? Diebold is a registered trademark of Diebold Corporation. Any other marks are the property of their respective owners."

FITRAKIS

Diebold, electronic voting and the vast right-wing conspiracy

The Governor of Ohio, Bob Taft, and other prominent state officials, commute to their downtown Columbus offices on Broad Street. This is the so-called "Golden Finger," the safe route through the majority black inner-city near east side. The Broad Street BP station, just east of downtown, is the place where affluent suburbanites from Bexley can stop, gas up, get their coffee and New York Times. Those in need of cash visit BP's Diebold manufactured CashSource+ ATM machine which provides a paper receipt of the transaction to all customers upon request.

Many of Taft's and President George W. Bush's major donors, like Diebold's current CEO Walden "Wally" O'Dell, reside in Columbus' northwest suburb Upper Arlington. O'Dell is on record stating that he is "committed to helping Ohio deliver its electoral votes to the President" this year. On September 26, 2003, he hosted an Ohio Republican Party fundraiser for Bush's re-election at his Cotswold Manor mansion. Tickets to the fundraiser cost $1000 per couple, but O'Dell's fundraising letter urged those attending to "Donate or raise $10,000 for the Ohio Republican Party."

According to the Columbus Dispatch: "Last year, O'Dell and his wife Patricia, campaigned for passage of two liquor options that made their portion of Tremont Road wet.

On November 5, Upper Arlington residents narrowly passed measures that allowed fundraising parties to offer more than beer, even though his 10,800-square-foot home is a residence, a permit is required because alcohol is included in the price of fundraising tickets. O'Dell is also allowed to serve "beer, wine and mixed drinks" at Sunday fundraisers.

O'Dell's fund-raising letter followed on the heels of a visit to President Bush's Crawford Texas ranch by "Pioneers and Rangers," the designation for people who had raised $100,000 or more for Bush's re-election.

If Ohio's Republican Secretary of State Kenneth Blackwell has his way, Diebold will receive a contract to supply touch screen electronic voting machines for much of the state. None of these Diebold machines will provide a paper receipt of the vote.

Diebold, located in North Canton, Ohio, does its primary business in ATM and ticket-vending machines. Critics of Diebold point out that virtually every other machine the company makes provides a paper trail to verify the machine's calculations. Oddly, only the voting machines lack this essential function.

State Senator Teresa Fedor of Toledo introduced Senate Bill 167 late last year mandating that every voting machine in Ohio generate a "voter verified paper audit trail." Secretary of State Blackwell has denounced any attempt to require a paper trail as an effort to "derail" election reform. Blackwell's political career is an interesting one: he emerged as a black activist in Cincinnati supporting municipal charter reform, became an elected Democrat, then an Independent, and now is a prominent Republican with his eyes on the Governor's mansion.

Voter fraud

A joint study by the California and Massachusetts Institutes of Technology following the 2000 election determined that between

1.5 and 2 million votes were not counted due to confusing paper ballots or faulty equipment. The federal government's solution to the problem was to pass the Help America Vote Act (HAVA) of 2002.

One of the law's stated goals was "Replacement of punch card and lever voting machines." The new voting machines would be high-tech touch screen computers, but if there's no paper trail, how do you know if there's been a computer glitch? How can the results be trusted? And how do you recount to see if the actual votes match the computer's tally?

Bev Harris, author of *Black Box Voting: Ballot Tampering in the 21st Century*, argues that without a paper trail, these machines are open to massive voter fraud. Diebold has already placed some 50,000 machines in 37 states and their track record is causing Harris, Johns Hopkins University professors and others great concern.

Johns Hopkins researchers at the Information Security Institute issued a report declaring that Diebold's electronic voting software contained "stunning flaws." The researchers concluded that vote totals could be altered at the voting machines and by remote access. Diebold vigorously refuted the Johns Hopkins report, claiming the researchers came to "a multitude of false conclusions."

Perhaps to settle the issue, apparently an insider leaked documents from the Diebold Election Systems website and posted internal documents from the company to Harris' website. Diebold went to court to stop, according to court records, the "wholesale reproduction" of some 13,000 pages of company material.

The Associated Press reported in November 2003 that: "Computer programmers, ISPs and students at [at] least 20 universities, including the University of California, Berkeley, and the Massachusetts Institute of Technology received cease and desist letters" from Diebold. A group of Swarthmore College students launched an "electronic civil disobedience" campaign to keep the hacked documents permanently posted on the Internet.

Harris writes that the documents expose how the mainstream

media reversed their call projecting Al Gore as winner of Florida after someone "subtracted 16,022 votes from Al Gore, and in still some undefined way, added 4000 erroneous votes to George W. Bush." Hours later, the votes were returned. One memo from Lana Hires of Global Election Systems, now Diebold, reads: "I need some answers! Our department is being audited by the County. I have been waiting for someone to give me an explanation as to why Precinct 216 gave Al Gore a minus 16,022 [votes] when it was uploaded." Another hacked internal memo, written by Talbot Iredale, Senior VP of Research and Development for Diebold Election Systems, documents "unauthorized" replacement votes in Volusia County.

Harris also uncovered a revealing 87-page CBS news report and noted, "According to CBS documents, the erroneous 20,000 votes in Volusia was directly responsible to calling the election for Bush." The first person to call the election for Bush was Fox election analyst John Ellis, who had the advantage of conferring with his prominent cousins George W. Bush and Florida Governor Jeb Bush.

Incestuous relationships

Increasingly, investigative writers seeking an explanation have looked to Diebold's history for clues. The electronic voting industry is dominated by only a few corporations – Diebold, Election Systems & Software (ES&S) and Sequoia. Diebold and ES&S combined count an estimated 80% of U.S. black box electronic votes.

In the early 1980s, brothers Bob and Todd Urosevich founded ES&S's originator, Data Mark. The brothers Urosevich obtained financing from the far-Right Ahmanson family in 1984, which purchased a 68% ownership stake, according to the Omaha World Herald. After brothers William and Robert Ahmanson infused Data Mark with new capital, the name was changed to American Information Systems (AIS). California newspapers have long documented the Ahmanson family's ties to right-wing evangelical Christian and Republican circles.

In 2001, the Los Angeles Times reported, ". . . primarily funded by evangelical Christians – particularly the wealthy Ahmanson family of Irvine – the [Discovery] institute's $1-million annual program has produced 25 books, a stream of conferences and more than 100 fellowships for doctoral and postdoctoral research." The chief philanthropists of the Discovery Institute, that pushes creationist science and education in California, are Howard and Roberta Ahmanson.

According to Group Watch, in the 1980s Howard F. Ahmanson, Jr. was a member of the highly secretive far-Right Council for National Policy, an organization that included Lieutenant Colonel Oliver North, Major General John K. Singlaub and other Iran-Contra scandal notables, as well as former Klan members like Richard Shoff. Ahmanson, heir to a savings and loan fortune, is little reported on in the mainstream U.S. press. But, English papers like The Independent are a bit more forthcoming on Ahmanson's politics.

"On the right, figures such as Richard Mellon Scaife and Howard Ahmanson have given hundreds of millions of dollars over several decades to political projects both high (setting up the Heritage Foundation think-tank, the driving engine of the Reagan presidency) and low (bankrolling investigations into President Clinton's sexual indiscretions and the suicide of the White House insider Vincent Foster)," wrote The Independent last November.

The Sunday Mail described an individual as, ". . . a fundamentalist Christian more in the mould of U.S. multi-millionaire Howard Ahmanson, Jr., who uses his fortune to promote so-called traditional family values . . . by waving fortunes under their noses, Ahmanson has the ability to cajole candidates into backing his right-wing Christian agenda.

Ahmanson is also a chief contributor to the Chalcedon Institute that supports the Christian reconstruction movement. The movement's philosophy advocates, among other things, "mandating the death penalty for homosexuals and drunkards."

The Ahmanson family sold their shares in American Information Systems to the McCarthy Group and the World Herald Company, Inc. Republican Senator Chuck Hagel disclosed in public documents that he was the Chairman of American Information Systems and claimed between a $1 to 5 million investment in the McCarthy Group. In 1997, American Information Systems purchased Business Records Corp. (BRC), formerly Texas-based election company Cronus Industries, to become ES&S. One of the BRC owners was Carolyn Hunt of the right-wing Hunt oil family, which supplied much of the original money for the Council on National Policy.

In 1996, Hagel became the first elected Republican Nebraska senator in 24 years when he did surprisingly well in an election where the votes were verified by the company he served as chairman and maintained a financial investment. In both the 1996 and 2002 elections, Hagel's ES&S counted an estimated 80% of his winning votes. Due to the contracting out of services, confidentiality agreements between the State of Nebraska and the company kept this matter out of the public eye. Hagel's first election victory was described as a "stunning upset" by one Nebraska newspaper.

Hagel's official biography states, "Prior to his election to the U.S. Senate, Hagel worked in the private sector as the President of McCarthy and Company, an investment banking firm based in Omaha, Nebraska and served as Chairman of the Board of American Information Systems." During the first Bush presidency, Hagel served as Deputy Director and Chief Operating Officer of the 1990 Economic Summit of Industrialized Nations (G-7 Summit).

Bob Urosevich was the Programmer and CEO at AIS, before being replaced by Hagel. Bob now heads Diebold Election Systems and his brother Todd is a top executive at ES&S. Bob created Diebold's original electronic voting machine software. Thus, the brothers Urosevich, originally funded by the far Right, figure in the counting of approximately 80% of electronic voting in the United States.

Like Ohio, the State of Maryland was disturbed by the potential for massive electronic voter fraud. The voters of that state were reassured when the state hired SAIC to monitor Diebold's system.

Admiral Bill Owens was with the company. Owens served as a military aide to both Vice President Dick Cheney and former Defense Secretary Frank Carlucci, who now works with George H.W. Bush at the controversial Carlyle Group. Robert Gates, former CIA Director and close friend of the Bush family, served on the SAIC Board.

Diebold's track record

Wherever Diebold and ES&S go, irregularities and historic Republican upsets follow. Alastair Thompson, writing for scoop.co of New Zealand, explored whether or not the 2002 U.S. mid-term elections were "fixed by electronic voting machines supplied by Republican-affiliated companies." The scoop investigation concluded that: "The state where the biggest upset occurred, Georgia, is also the state that ran its election with the most electronic voting machines." Those machines were supplied by Diebold.

Wired News reported that ". . . a former worker in Diebold's Georgia warehouse says the company installed patches on its machine before the state's 2002 gubernatorial election that were never certified by independent testing authorities or cleared with Georgia election officials." Questions were raised in Texas when three Republican candidates in Comal County each received exactly the same number of votes – 18,181 – on ES&S machines.

Following the 2003 California election, an audit of the company revealed that Diebold Election Systems voting machines installed uncertified software in all 17 counties using its equipment.

Former CIA Station Chief John Stockwell writes that one of the favorite tactics of the CIA during the Reagan-Bush administration in the 1980s was to control countries by manipulating the election process. "CIA apologists leap up and say, 'Well, most of these things are not so bloody.' And that's true. You're giving politicians some money so he'll throw his party in this direction or that one, or make false speeches on your behalf, or something like that. It may be non-violent, but it's still illegal intervention in other country's affairs, raising the question of whether or not we're going to have a world in which laws, rules of behavior are respected," Stockwell wrote. Documents illustrate that the Reagan and Bush administration supported computer manipulation in both Noriega's rise to power in Panama and in Marcos' attempt to retain power in the Philippines. Many of the Reagan administration's staunchest supporters were members of the Council on National Policy.

The perfect solution

Ohio Senator Fedor continues to fight valiantly for Senate Bill 167 and the Holy Grail of the "voter verified paper audit trail." Proponents of a paper trail were emboldened when Athan Gibbs, President and CEO of TruVote International, demonstrated a voting machine at a vendor's fair in Columbus that provides two separate voting receipts.

The first paper receipt displays the voter's touch screen selection under plexiglass that falls into a lockbox after the voter approves. Also, the TruVote system provides the voter with a receipt that includes a unique voter ID and pin number which can be used to call in to a voter audit internet connection to make sure the vote cast was actually counted.

Brooks Thomas, Coordinator of Elections in Tennessee, stated, "I've not seen anything that compares to the Gibbs' TruVote validation system. . . ." The Assistant Secretary of State of Georgia, Terrel L. Slayton, Jr., claimed Gibbs had come up with the "perfect solution."

Still, there remains opposition from Ohio Secretary of State Blackwell. His spokesperson Carlo LoParo recently pointed out that federal mandates under HAVA do not require a paper trail: ". . . if Congress changes the federal law to require it [a paper trail], we'll certainly make that a requirement of our efforts." LoParo went on to accuse advocates of a paper trail of attempting to "derail" voting reform.

U.S. Representative Rush Holt introduced HR 2239, The Voter Confidence and Increased Accessibility Act of 2003, that would require electronic voting machines to produce a paper trail so that voters may verify that their screen touches match their actual vote. Election officials would also have a paper trail for recounts.

As Blackwell pressures the Ohio legislature to adopt electronic voting machines without a paper trail, Athan Gibbs wonders, "Why would you buy a voting machine from a company like Diebold which provides a paper trail for every single machine it makes except its voting machines? And then, when you ask it to verify its numbers, it hides behind 'trade secrets.'"

Maybe the Diebold decision makes sense, if you believe, to paraphrase Henry Kissinger, that democracy is too important to leave up to the votes of the people.

February 24, 2004

FITRAKIS

On Bush, drugs and hypocrisy

When President George W. Bush signed the Drug-Free Communities Act in 2002, he asserted, "If you quit drugs, you join the fight against terror in America." During the 2002 Superbowl, in the aftermath of 9/11, Bush's Office of National Drug Control Policy aired two TV ads asking the simple question, "Where do terrorists get their money?" The answer: "If you buy drugs, some of it might come from you."

Many marijuana activists have argued that growing your own weed is counterterrorist activity. Still, this line of thinking concedes Bush's simple-minded assertion.

The better response to the terrorist money question should be from Friends and Family of Bush (FOBs). The terrorist network responsible for 9/11 was primarily financed by opium profits from the Golden Crescent where Afghanistan, Pakistan and Iran come together. The Reagan and Bush administration policy was to allow the opium lords to launder their drug money through the Bank of Credit and Commerce International (BCCI) as long as some of the proceeds went to finance the fight against the Soviet Union. Ironically, all of this is documented in a Senate Report, "The BCCI Affair," chaired by Senator John Kerry.

The Bush family is close friends with Texas' Bath brothers.
James R. Bath was an investor in George W.'s Arbusto Oil Company. Bath was also an investor in BCCI. The Senate Report also documents that Sheikh Abdullah Bahksh of Saudi Arabia not only held 16% of the stock of Harken Energy, a company that later bought up George W.'s Spectrum 7 oil company, but also was a key investor in BCCI. George H.W. Bush, former director of the CIA, maintained ties with BCCI despite its narcotics trafficking during both the 1970s and 80s.

Legal documents show that James Bath served as the U.S. business representative for Salem bin Laden, brother of Osama, beginning in 1976, the same year that George the Elder took over the directorship of the CIA.

So, where did the terrorist money come from? The   FOBs. A good book on the subject is False Profits: The Inside Story of BCCI, the World's Most Corrupt Financial Empire, by Peter Truell of the Wall Street Journal, and Larry Gurwin, award-winning business reporter. Another resource is Chapter eleven: "Making Afghanistan Safe for Opium" of Alexander Cockburn's and Jeffrey St. Clair's Whiteout: The CIA, Drugs and the Press.

Cynics might sneer that these connections are pre-1991, when Osama bin Laden broke with his CIA allies. Yet, the Bush family's relationship with opium runners remains odd. Initially, Bush the Younger's administration gave Afghanistan's Taliban $43 million to eradicate opium crops. The fact that the Taliban was harboring Osama and were one of the most repressive regimes on Earth did not sit well with critics.

Following September 11, 2001, however, the Bush administration's drug policy toward Afghanistan changed dramatically. The UN issued a report documenting continued opium production in Afghanistan and advised the U.S.-led coalition to act quickly to destroy the bumper crop of opium. The UN report determined that: "Afghanistan has been the main source of illicit opium: 70 percent of global illicit opium production in 2000 and up to 90 percent of heroin in European drug markets originated from Afghanistan."

"The global importance of the ban on opium poppy cultivation and trafficking in Afghanistan is enormous," concluded the UN report.

Charles R. Smith, writing for NewsMax.com, reported the grumblings from anonymous sources on Capitol Hill in late March 2002 when the Bush administration reversed its policy and decided not to push for the destruction of Afghanistan's opium crops. The CIA argued that the destruction of the opium crop might destabilize General Pervez Musharraf's Pakistani government. After all, Americans wouldn't want that.

Musharraf is everything that Saddam longed to be, but could never accomplish. He's a military dictator referred to by the American mainstream press as a "self-appointed" president. He has nuclear weapons; he harbors an effective terrorist network including Osama bin Laden and key Al Qaeda figures; he's responsible for giving North Korea radioactive material to build their nuclear bombs; and despite all of this, he is still a friend of the U.S. and, more importantly, a FOB. By the way, scientists in his government offered Saddam Hussein nuclear material, which the Iraqi leader turned down, according to The New York Times.

Who are we to challenge the CIA? Wasn't it necessary for them to allow their Contra allies to run cocaine into the United States in the 1980s? Wasn't it the height of patriotism when they allowed Air America to transport opium into U.S. military bases in the 1960s and 70s? But all that concerned the Cold War, national security and geopolitical strategy.

But what about the President's own actions in the war against drugs? In 1999, our President has steadfastly maintained that he hadn't done cocaine in the last seven years, no wait, fifteen years, or possibly since 1974, all reported in Time magazine. As Governor of Texas, he announced that people "need to know that drug use has consequences." Apparently, bad memory may be one of those consequences. As governor, Bush signed legislation that authorized judges to sentence first-time offenders with less than a gram of cocaine to a maximum 180 days in jail instead of automatic probation.

During the height of the notorious   Blowgate scandal, George W. scrambled back to his ancestral home in Columbus, Ohio to proclaim "I'm going to tell people I made mistakes and that I've learned from my mistakes." His mistakes most likely cost him his flight status in the National Guard when he failed to take a medical exam following the military's adoption of a mandatory drug testing policy.

If hemp activists want to stop the insane and authoritarian War on Drugs, they've got to admit their mistakes. The movement's biggest problem appears to be lack of connections with the CIA, bin Laden, the Bush family and other known terrorists.

April 15, 2004

CLASS WAR

WASSERMAN

Bush to veterans: Drop Dead

As another Veteran's Day passes by, George W. Bush has sent a clear and present message to the men and women of America's armed forces: Drop Dead.

In an astonishing series of cynical attacks on veterans rights, benefits and sanctity, the administration has shortchanged our military personnel on their medical care, pensions, compensation for having been tortured, access to vital information about health dangers suffered in service, and even their body armor.

After promising that the Iraqi people would be "dancing in the streets" upon their arrival, US troops are being attacked up to three dozen times a day. In response, Bush has imposed an unprecedented media blackout on coverage of their corpses coming home.

Bush himself has yet to attend the funeral of any soldier slain in Iraq. But he has attacked those within the military who would express a democratic opinion against his policies.

Bush has also violated a crucial national tradition---dating to George Washington---against a Chief Executive appearing in military garb while in civilian office.

Bush himself went AWOL from his Alabama National Guard unit during the Vietnam War. His lengthy absence may have made him technically a deserter, and thus subject to prosecution, which has never happened.

Earlier this year Bush was flown by military jet onto the aircraft carrier Abraham Lincoln. Strutting on the flight deck in a photo op jump flight suit, he spoke before a "Mission Accomplished" banner which he now denies was rigged by his handlers. Bush has publicly cited his alleged "combat" experience, but never served in any battle. He showed his tactical genius by daring the Iraqi resistance to "bring it on," followed by the deaths of scores of soldiers and civilians.

Three supreme US generals who did serve in wartime--- Washington, Ulysses S. Grant and Dwight Eisenhower---have also served as US president. To emphasize the crucial separation of the military from American civilian government, all made a point of avoiding public appearances in military uniform while in office. So have other veteran presidents such as John F. Kennedy and Bush's father, George H.W. Bush.

But George W. Bush soiled that tradition with a Tom Cruise routine that cost taxpayers at least $800,000, and may have deprived the crew of the U.S.S. Lincoln of a day's leave.

This Veteran's Day, Bush signed the Fallen Patriots Tax Relief Act, which doubles the tax-free death gratuity payment given to the families of fallen soldiers from $6,000 to $12,000. He also approved the National Cemetery Expansion Act to help establish new military burial grounds.

But he has now frozen $1 billion in financial settlements won by 17 U.S. combat veterans who were whipped, beaten, burned, electrically shocked and starved by Saddam Hussein during the 1991 Persian Gulf War. The vets and their families filed for compensation under a 1996 law, citing the Geneva Convention.

On July 7, U.S. District Judge Richard Roberts ordered Iraq to pay the 17 ex-POWs and their families $653 million in compensatory damages, plus another $306 million in punitive damages. But Bush has cited "weighty foreign policy interests" and has sued to withhold the money.

Meanwhile Secretary of Defense Donald   Rumsfeld has blatantly violated a 1990s law requiring the military to keep baseline medical data so the health of the US soldiers now serving in Iraq can be properly monitored. The demand derives from Gulf War Syndrome, which may have caused disabling diseases among as many as 220,000 vets. But Rumsfeld has ignored the law.

The Administration is also denying service women access to reproductive care, including abortions. And it has failed to provide body armor to some forty percent of the soldiers serving in Iraq.

Meanwhile Bush has fought to slash long-standing benefits due surviving veterans of the World Wars, Korea and Vietnam. The GOP has opposed repealing the Disabled Veterans Tax, which mandated that money due some 600,000 surviving vets in disability pay be deducted, dollar-for-dollar. At one point Rumsfeld told the White House to veto the Defense Appropriations Bill if it gave the vets that money.

A firestorm of outrage has forced the administration into a compromise phased in over ten years. But it will still deny thousands of veterans their benefits as they die off.

With the relentless militarization of the mainstream media, Bush clearly believes he can ignore the soldiers he will condemn to death, disease and abject poverty.

Especially now that he has announced his courageous support for more cemeteries in which to bury their unphotographed corpses.

November 12, 2003

Behind every Bush there's a scandal

So, Kevin Phillips' thesis in his new book American Dynasty, is that the Bush family are long-standing war profiteers, Machiavellians and a WASP clan of financial hustlers. To be fair to the Bush family and to test Phillips' thesis, the Free Press decided to investigate what a lesser-known Bush brother was up to recently. Neil Bush was our choice, since we figured he would be repentant after his embarrassing involvement as a director of the defunct Silverado Savings and Loan in Denver during the 1980s.

Recall that Neil, as a bank director, had a conflict of interest problem after voting to approve loans totaling $132 million from Silverado to his business partners. His partners, in turn, loaned him hundreds of thousands of dollars, which he only had to pay back if he made a profit. His punishment was banishment from investment banking for life. Of course, he did have that little problem after Silverado. According to the Dayton Daily News, he got a $2 million loan from the Small Business Association and "walked on it."

Still, how bad could Neil be? He wasn't orchestrating coups in Florida like brother Jeb; he didn't lie to the whole world and wage a criminally aggressive wars to steal oil like George W.; and he didn't benefit from the U.S. Patriot Act like brother Marvin P. Bush, who became a cofounder in Winston Partners, a firm investing in outsourcing offshore information technology (surveillance and spying, for short).

Perhaps Phillips had a point that the family is prone to nepotism, when it turned out that Neil was targeting schools in Florida to buy software from his company, Ignite. First, Florida Governor Jeb Bush made education testing a key component of his administration's educational policy. Then the Associated Press (AP) exposed that Neil was peddling his test preparation software at $30 per Florida student. Who knows Neil's motives? He might have just been trying to help deprived inner city children prepare for racially and culturally biased standardized exams.

Shocking revelations about Neil's business and sex life made headlines last November. According to Neil's own testimony in his divorce proceedings, he was in a semiconductor manufacturing business deal with the son of former Communist Chinese President Jiang Zemin. Their company, Grace Semiconductor Manufacturing Corporation promised to pay Neil $2 million in stock over five years for his work as a consultant and director. Neil admits he didn't do much consulting or directing, but anonymous women kept coming to his hotel room in Taiwan and Hong Kong, knocking on his door and then having sex with him.

When his wife's attorney asked him under oath: "Mr. Bush, you have to admit it's a pretty remarkable thing for a man just to go to a hotel room door, and open it, and have a woman standing there and have sex with her." Neil displayed that legendary Bush honesty by admitting, "It was very unusual."

Neil also admitted that it was "correct" to conclude that he had ". . . absolutely no educational background in semiconductors. . ."

In January, the AP reported that Neil made at least $171,370 in one day by exercising stock options in a small U.S. high-tech firm. Neil claims that "my timing on this transaction was very fortunate" in reference to a July 19, 1999 purchase and quick sale of stock in Kopin Corp. of Taunton, Massachusetts. The sale, coincidentally, came on a day that the company's stock priced soared after the company announced it had acquired a new Asian client.

Cashing in on a same morning quick stock buy and sell before the market crash is just another example of that blind Bush luck.

No insider information here, like that nasty Martha Stewart. Just good old-fashioned Wall Street casino gambling, Texas-style. Bush was mum about whether his stock option came with sex from anonymous women. After all, he's a family values guy.

February 21, 2004

WASSERMAN

Bush wins Triple Trifecta as worst president ever

"The worst president in our lifetime" is how many Americans view George W. Bush.

But Bush is not merely the worst president in recent memory. He's the worst in all US history. And he's won the distinction not on a weakness or two, but in at least nine separate categories, giving him a triple trifecta.

It's a record unmatched by any previous president.

Let's count the ways:

TRIFECTA ONE: Economy, Environment, Education

Economy:

Until now, Herbert Hoover has been the president most closely associated with economic disaster. He presided over the 1929 stock crash, and choked while the economy collapsed around him.

Bush did not preside over the 2000   Nasdaq crash. But he's turned the biggest federal surplus into history's biggest deficit, which a nervous global banking community sees as a potential weapon of mass fiscal destruction. Bush has lost more jobs than Hoover. A top Bush advisor has called outsourcing "just a new way of doing international trade."

Bush has achieved the economic   trifecta by simultaneously collapsing the dollar while gutting the industrial infrastructure and running up gargantuan trade deficits. Even GOP conservatives are petrified over a Bush Blowout that could make the 1930s seem a time of widespread prosperity. With Vice President Dick Cheney saying "deficits don't matter," the administration has introduced a form of "kamikaze economics" entirely new to the American presidency.

Environment:

Bush's "No Tree Left Standing" attack on Mother Earth has transcended even Ronald Reagan's all-out anti-green assault. More people will ultimately die from the resulting climate chaos, toxic emissions and other eco-fallout than from anything Al Queda could imagine.

Simply put, Bush has trashed not only eco-progress dating back to Richard Nixon, but also the achievements of both Roosevelts, scorching the earth all the way back to US Grant and Yellowstone, our first national park, now being Bushwhacked.

Education:

Bush's "No Child Left Behind" scam has imposed massive new costs on state and local school systems with no tangible payback. Even Utah has just said no. Even Reagan's slash and burn of public education has been trumped by an administration for whom the three R's are "Religion, Reaction, and Revelations."

TRIFECTA TWO: Corruption, Constitution, Global Contempt

Corruption:

Until Bush, the friends of Warren G. Harding were the kings of White House sleaze. Nixon and Reagan's made a serious challenge. But with Enron, Halliburton, Bechtel and other Bush funders profiting from the slaughter in Iraq and the decimation of the electric grid and the natural environment, W has captured the crown of public theft.

Constitution:

Richard Nixon's repressive attack on the Vietnam anti-war movement outstripped even the Red Scare excesses of Woodrow Wilson after World War I and those of John Adams after the

Revolution. But Bush and Attorney-General John Ashcroft have shredded the Bill of Rights with unprecedented glee. From the Patriot Act, Homeland Security and an escalated drug war, Bush has become George Orwell's Big Brother, making Nixon look like a civil libertarian.

Global Contempt:

American presidents from Washington to Lincoln to FDR to JFK have been loved around the world. Jimmy Carter, now an ambassador for peace, may have excited the most global contempt by preaching human rights while embracing the brutal Shah of Iran.

But no American president has incited such worldwide hatred as George W. Bush. He has turned the global sympathy from the 9/11 terror attacks into inexpressible rage over the attack on Afghanistan and Iraq, his contempt for the United Nations and his cynical, uncaring arrogance and global ignorance. By blatantly lying to both the United Nations and in the State of the Union, and then unleashing brutal violence, Bush has become the most polarizing president in US history abroad as well as at home.

TRIFECTA THREE: Military madness, Messianic delusion, Macho Matricide

Military Madness:

About a dozen US presidents served in the armed forces. Three---Washington, Grant and Eisenhower---are among history's greatest generals. None ever advocated attacking countries that have not attacked us. All honored the firewall between military and civilian rule by avoiding wearing a military uniform while in office.

Bush trashed that tradition with his infamous flight suit.   Bill Clinton occupied the short list of presidents known to have dodged the draft. But with an entire cabinet of chickenhawks, Bush gets the Congressional medal for having used his wealth and connections to avoid military service, for likely having gone AWOL and for lying about having ever been in combat. None has heaped such hypocritical praise on American soldiers while slashing their benefits.

Messianic Delusion:

Presidents from Washington to Lincoln to the   Roosevelts to Reagan have invoked the name of God. Only Bush claims to speak directly to Him and for Him.   Only Bush claims to have been elected by Him (the American people certainly didn't do it).

At least since the witch trials of Salem in the 1690s, no other president has ever attempted to impose his personal religion on the nation---or world---as has Bush.

Macho Matricide:

Ronald Reagan ostensibly opposed a women's right to choose, but did little about it. Ditto George H.W. Bush.

But W. has launched an unprecedented crusade against women's rights, affirmative action and a whole range of social legislation supporting equality between the races, genders, communities of preference and classes.

Much more could be said. These modest nine points omit Bush's attacks on organized labor, health insurance, retirement benefits, renewable energy and much much more.

But if you ever have a pinge of doubt about Shrub being the worst president ever, just repeat the phrase "Triple Trifecta" three times. Then go out and organize, organize, organize.

February 16, 2004

AMERICAN MASS TRANSIT

WASSERMAN

Bush's hole-in-head nuke cronies re-open door for terror apocalypse

George W. Bush's big-money backers at Ohio's infamous FirstEnergy electric monopoly are re-opening the door for a nuclear apocalypse by terror or incompetence (whichever comes first). In classic Bush style, they are trashing public oversight as they go.

The Akron-based FirstEnergy blacked out the entire northeast a year ago, resulting in at least $10 billion in losses to the public. No criminal charges have been filed, though the company has reportedly paid tens of millions in civil suits and has been under grand jury investigation for a wide range of issues.

FirstEnergy's top management, starting with President Anthony Alexander, has poured huge sums into Bush's campaign coffers. Before last year's blackout FE big wigs hosted a fundraiser with Vice President Dick Cheney, raising a reported $600,000.

FirstEnergy has gouged billions from Ohio ratepayers as part of a California-style deregulation fiasco. In its wake, FE extended its reach from northern Ohio to New Jersey, buying the Three Mile Island nuke plant along the way. Promised competition has not materialized, leaving more than four million FE customers hostage to an unregulated monopoly.

FirstEnergy has so badly mismanaged the Perry reactor on Lake Erie East of Cleveland that the timid, industry-owned Nuclear Regulatory Commission has actually threatened to shut it down. Repeated, extremely dangerous pump failures have prompted a rare admission of guilt from the utility itself.

FE also owns the infamous Davis-Besse reactor outside Toledo. Over a six-year period boric acid leaked on D-B's critical reactor pressure vessel, eating a six-inch hole all the way through it. Only a thin shroud and what one expert calls "blind luck" saved all of northern Ohio from a radioactive apocalypse.

The aging, badly built Three Mile Island clone is notoriously vulnerable to terror attack. Recent breakthroughs in windpower have made it possible for northern Ohioans to entirely supplant the rickety reactor with new turbines. Two large wind machines went on line near Bowling Green last September and are running ahead of projections; two more are on their way up.

While D-B was shut for repairs for more than a year, the region suffered no shortages. The reactors on line during last August's blackout worsened rather than lessened the crisis.

The Washington-based Nuclear Information & Resource Service is challenging recent NRC rulings allowing D-B to restart after a fresh round of safety and operating problems. On the afternoon of Monday, August 16, three NRC Commissioners quietly voted to hold a public meeting at 9:25am the following morning. The meeting was part of a legal appeal against the Commission's vote on restart. NRC rules require a one-week notice.

Instead the Commissioners e-mailed notice to NIRS attorneys in Toledo at 8:30 the morning of August 17th, less than an hour before the hearing was to begin. "The Agency sunset its own sunshine law," says NIRS's Paul Gunter. "Whose government is this, anyway?"

U.S. Representative Dennis Kucinich (D-Cleveland) has called FE's performance "troubling." NIRS had planned to call him and

Representative Marcy Kaptur (D-Toledo) to underscore growing northern Ohio determination to get these reactors shut. In objecting to the Davis-Besse restart, NIRS and local plaintiffs have documented violations of mandatory fire protection for reactor safe shutdown equipment. According to Gunter, FE's fire protection plan relies on "Indiana Jones-style runners" instead of reliable structural firewalls.

Critics also warn the shaky, unstable reactor could be a target for terror attack. A disaster at Davis-Besse or Perry could cause untold casualties along the Erie lakefront, along with incalculable billions in economic damage.

But Toledo Attorney Terry Lodge   charges that "when serious safety allegations didn't fit the agency's restart script, NRC omitted them from any restart considerations."

Plaintiff Michael Keegan called the NRC "rogues masquerading as regulators" and demanded Congressional intervention.

Given FE's lucrative ties to the Bush Administration, and the fact that they've walked away unindicted from last year's blackout, only a regime change in Washington is likely to have an impact.

August 20, 2004

WASSERMAN

The Cheney-Bush energy disaster is about to come to a vote

Editor's note: This bill went down in defeat.

As would be expected in the Age of Bush, an energy bill that will affect all Americans for decades to come, and cost us hundreds of billions of dollars, is being hashed out in secret. It's a direct off-shoot of those notorious secret meetings held by Vice President Dick Cheney, about which he refuses to disclose anything, despite a string of court orders. A final Congressional vote may come this week.

For New Englanders, it will mean critical shortages of natural gas within the very near future, plus soaring oil prices and escalating danger from nuclear power plants -Vermont Yankee, Pilgrim, Seabrook and the two Millstone reactors still operating in Connecticut.

The "Senator from Big Nuke"---Pete Domenici of New Mexico---is working with the "Rep. from Big Oil"---W.J. "Billy" Tauzin of Louisiana---to cook up legislation that will mean billions in benefits to their big campaign donors and a nightmare of environmental, health and social costs to the rest of us, for generations to come.

These two fossil-nuke flunkies have taken control of the Senate-House conference committee, giving them a free hand to concoct a gargantuan handout of taxpayer money and environmental resources to their principle campaign contributors.

Domenici is working up the nuclear power subsidies. His original plan was for at least $8.5 billion in guaranteed loans for new reactor construction. He's not saying right now whether he's upped the ante even further. But the bill does extend the Price-Anderson liability shield, letting reactor builders escape financial responsibility for a catastrophic meltdown. It would hand the industry another $2 billion for "research and development," plus another $865 million for failed reprocessing technologies and yet another $1.1 billion for a worthless Advanced Hydrogen Reactor Co-generation Project.

The bill also weakens whistle-blower protections as well as prohibitions against exporting radioactive materials, which could be made into bombs.

The bill repeals the Public Utility Holding Company Act (PUHCA), a New Deal mainstay that has prevented even more Enron-style disasters. Repeal would guarantee them.

The bill would give power of eminent domain to the Federal Energy Regulatory Commission (FERC), eliminating state and local control over power-line construction.

It would also alter the FERC's "just and reasonable" rate setting guideline, letting transmission line owners gouge consumers still further.

For the oil and gas barons, the list of goodies is almost endless from massive subsidies tax breaks and rebates to opening vast tracts of scenic and ecologically vital areas for exploitation and ruin. There are exemptions from the Safe Water Drinking Act and the Clean Water Act. There are no substantial gains for auto fuel efficiency.

There is also no Renewable Portfolio Standard (RPS), the widely popular requirement that a percentage of the nation's electricity be generated with wind or solar power. And there are no concessions for escalating carbon dioxide emissions linked to global warming.

Taken as a whole, the Cheney-Bush energy bill is a prescription for economic and ecological catastrophe. Senator Jim Jeffords of Vermont has put forward a reasonable alternative in his Electric Reliability Security Act.

But Bush wants legislation that will virtually guarantee future blackouts, nuclear meltdowns, skyrocketing fossil fuel prices and catastrophic ecological disease.

The tragedy is that wind power is now cheaper, safer, cleaner and more reliable than anything offered in this bill. There are some production tax credits for the wind industry. But they pale in comparison to what a sane energy plan would provide. Aid to solar power is virtually non-existent. Conservation and efficiency are, in the Age of Bush, considered too un-manly to even discuss.

In short, this is the energy plan from Hell. Dick Cheney and the coal/oil/nuke/gas industries that own him drafted it in secret. It deserves to die a speedy death. Call your Senators and Representatives today. Or you, your children and your children's children will pay a horrific price.

November 1, 2003

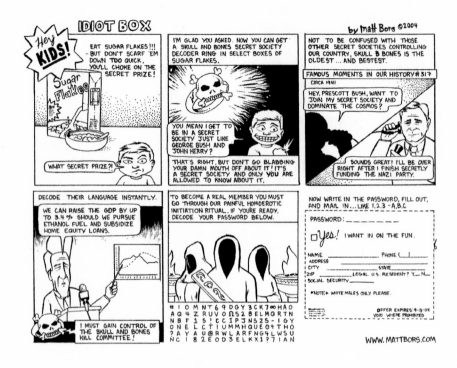

WWW.MATTBORS.COM

Rods from Gods: The insanity of Star Wars, the sequel

The lasting legacy of Ronald Wilson Reagan will be Star Wars and a bloated imperialist U.S. military budget. At the beginning of the recent war against Iraq, nearly two dozen years after Reagan first took office, his impact was plainly clear: the mainstream media pointed out that the U.S. military was estimated to be stronger than Rome at the height of her imperialism and stronger than Nazi Germany in 1940.

Reagan, starring in "The Return of the Cold War," doubled President Carter's military budget, increasing it from $145 billion to $290 billion in his first year. The Reagan-Bush Administration spent $1.5 trillion in their first five years, the largest military build-up during peacetime ever recorded. Star Wars was funded to the tune of tens of billions of dollars with the stated goal of nuclearizing space. But we were promised if the Soviet Union caved in there would be the mythical "peace dividend." Americans would benefit from a much smaller military budget.

Then Bush the Elder assumed the Presidency and ushered in the first Gulf War, and the military budget remained at Cold War levels. With the fall of the Soviet Union and the election of Bill Clinton, a modest decrease in the defense budget placed it in the $270 billion range. Both Bush the Elder and Clinton allowed the Star Wars funding to lag. Now Bush the Younger has resurrected the dream of U.S. dominance of the Earth via the militarization of space.

According to *Jane's Defense Weekly* , when the U.S. recently attacked Iraq, the Iraqi defense spending was $1 billion. The "axis of evil," defined in President Bush's January 2002 State of the Union address to include North Korea and Iran in addition to Iraq, had an estimated defense spending totaling $7 billion at the time. While the official rhetoric of the Bush administration still attempts in the most cynical fashion to portray the U.S. military as a force for good in the world, this old school propaganda is crashing beneath the weight of a $400 billion defense budget, soon to be half a trillion dollars. Moreover, public records, government websites and popular magazines tell the world that our real objective is "full spectrum dominance" of the planet.

The June issue of *Popular Science* spells out the future of the U.S. military in a cover story entitled, "Is This What War Will Come To?" Not surprisingly, the cover includes the words "Defense 2020: The Pentagon's Weapons of the Future." This is a reference to the U.S. military's directed energy program under the U.S. Space Command, known as "Joint Vision 2020." This is where you'll find the stated policy of the U.S. military -- "full spectrum dominance" of our planet.

"The projectile leaves the barrel at hypersonic velocity – Mach 7-plus – exits the Earth's atmosphere, re-enters under satellite guidance and lands on the building less than six minutes later; its incredible velocity vaporizes the target with kinetic energy alone."

Or, if you prefer, your tax dollars are building "a laser cannon that blasts from the air." There's also the phallic "Rods from Gods." These are "space-launched darts that strike like meteors." Paling in comparison is, "A gun that fires a million rounds a minute." The casual and open nature of the reporting in *Popular Science* stands in sharp contrast to the network news that insists on parroting and giving credibility to the Bush propaganda that the U.S. is promoting peace. We've gone from Reagan's slogan of "Peace through Strength" to the less subtle "America Uber Alles."

Central Ohio, as usual, is involved in this military madness. Lieutenant Colonel JoAnn Erno, head of the power division at the Air Force Resource Laboratory at Wright-Patterson Air Force Base, is quoted on the development of "tactical lasers."

But the *Popular Science* article is merely a part of a much greater military plan, which includes "using 'weather as a force multiplier'" and controlling the weather for military purposes by the year 2025. In April 1997, President Clinton's Defense Secretary William Cohen remarked at a terrorist conference at the University of Georgia, "Others are engaging even in an eco-type of terrorism whereby they can alter the climate, set off earthquakes, volcanoes remotely through the use of electromagnetic waves."

How does Cohen know this, and why hasn't the mainstream media seized upon the abundance of information in the public record regarding this terrorist threat?

Cohen knew it to be true because the so-called terrorists are emulating our own military tactics, they're just doing it on the cheap a la 'dirty bombs." To expose these new unimaginably powerful weapons of mass destruction would indict the United States as a ruthless high-tech imperialist power.

At the crux of the U.S. directed energy program is the High-frequency Active Auroral Research Program (HAARP) operating in Gakona, Alaska. This ionosphere agitator is the ultimate weapon of mass destruction. While the government officially denies its military application, Dr. Arnold Barnes of Phillips Lab lectured on the military applications of HAARP at the United States Army's Developmental Test Command Symposium in 1997, where the good doctor also outlined the history of the U.S. military's involvement in "weather modification."

But these Star Wars weapons of mass destruction will not make us safer. Just as in Iraq, people will develop the means for "irregular warfare" against an arrogant and superior military power, just as our founders did against the British. And if you don't believe me, you might want to consult the September 2001 issue of *Popular Mechanics* that tells us how anti-U.S. terrorists can build "electromagnetic bombs" that "could throw civilization back 200 years." The cost: "terrorists can build them for $400."

The illusion that the U.S. is anything other than new Roman imperialism, a demented high-tech Christian crusade, or a budding Fourth Reich with better PR cannot be hidden from the reality of the massive U.S. military budget and its born-again Star Wars program.

June 24, 2004

SUPPLY SIDE JOURNALISM

WASSERMAN

Rock & radiation, not Ronald Reagan, brought down the Kremlin

No greater nonsense will accompany Ronald Reagan to his grave than the idea that he brought down the Soviet Union and ended the Cold War.

Among the many causes of Soviet collapse two words stand out, and they aren't Ronald Reagan.

They are rock and radiation.

The GOP military's 1980s attempt to "spend the Soviets into oblivion" certainly feathered the nests of the defense contractors who contributed to Reagan's campaigns here, and who still fatten George W. Bush. Lockheed-Martin, Halliburton and an unholy host of GOP insiders have scored billions in profits from Iran-Contra to Star Wars to Desert Storm to Iraq.

But these were not the people who brought down the Kremlin. If anything, they prolonged Soviet rule with the unifying threat of apocalyptic attack.

No, it was rock & roll that wrecked the USSR. From the late 1960s on, the steady beat of the Beatles and Motown, Bob Dylan and Jimi Hendrix, shattered Stalinism at its stodgy core.

Precisely the things most hated by the Reagan's rightist culture warriors here eroded and helped dissolve the old-time Soviet culture there. Beamed in by radio, smuggled in on records and tapes, the "youth music" was unstoppable.

When Mikhail Gorbachev announced Perestroika, it was at least in partial response to the irresistible subversion of the western counterculture. Rock and roll was doing to the remnants of Stalin's Russia what it had already done to Eisenhower's America.

The final blow came not from Ronald Reagan's beloved nuclear weapons, but from the Soviets' own Three Mile Island.

After Chernobyl Unit Four exploded on April 26, 1986, Swedish radiation monitors detected huge clouds of radiation pouring out of the Ukraine. Gorbachev lied about it. Critical days passed before his "open" regime acknowledged the catastrophe.

As apocalyptic radiation poured over their land and into their bodies, millions of Soviet citizens were infuriated to learn from sources outside their country how horrific the disaster really was--- and that their lives were in genuine danger. Cancer, birth defects, stillbirths and more soared out of control. Gorbachev's credibility was forever shattered.

Soon a staggering 800,000 draftees---"liquidators"--- were forced into deadly manual clean-up at the reactor site. The horrific maelstrom of resulting disease fed a fierce organization parallel to the US's Vietnam Vets Against the War that remains an uncompromising political force throughout the former Soviet Union.

With the fury aimed at Gorbachev came devastating economic fallout. Untold billions went to evacuate and quarantine the Chernobyl region. The costs are still escalating. The danger of a renewed melt-down still boils beneath the surface.

The epidemic of radiation-related diseases has also taken a huge psychological toll, with countless evacuees and victims---many of them children---still in pitiable condition.

Himself a pusher of atomic power since his "Death Valley Days" working for General Electric, Reagan never mentioned the devastating impacts of Chernobyl. He also never thanked the

Beatles.

But a cultural revolution and a nuclear malfunction cracked the Kremlin's core. Reagan's beloved Star Wars made his GOP buddies even richer. But it was rock and radiation that finally did in the Soviets.

June 10, 2004

Ronald Reagan: A legacy of crack and cheese

The mainstream media spent an entire week mythologizing Ronald Wilson Reagan. Why did the corporate for-profit media spend so much time creating a cult of personality around a former President with an estimated 105 IQ? Because the actual historical reality of Reagan's life are so shockingly reactionary you need the pageantry, majesty and imagery of a Hollywood-scripted finale to cover up the thousands of damning facts.

Reagan was a snitch during his Hollywood years. As Anthony Summers makes clear in his book Official and Confidential: The Secret Life of J. Edgar Hoover, the "Gipper" had his own code name – "T-10" – and regularly provided the FBI with information on Communists, real, imagined and manufactured. Victor Navasky's Naming Names documents as well how Reagan, then the head of the Screen Actors Guild, kept the FBI well informed about "disloyal" actors. During Reagan's Moscow Summit, the President met with Russian students to discuss communism and capitalism. In a speech too simple to be included in Communism for Idiots, the President dusted off his old theoretical writings from Reader's Digest and Boy's Life and told the students why Marx was evil and unbridled capitalism good.

As his B-actor career faded, Reagan became a mouthpiece for General Electric, one of the world's largest arms manufacturers. Reagan's one clear talent was the ability to read a Teleprompter or memorize his lines on the glories of free enterprise. While his skills were sub-par by Hollywood standards, he was able to parlay bad acting into good politics. Reagan understood the uncritical nature of the American public and their appetite for neo-American hokum. As E.L. Doctorow pointed out in his 1980 article, "The Rise of Ronald Reagan": "...his tenure as GE spokesman overlapped the years in which the great electrical industry price-fixing scandal was going on."

"While Reagan extolled the virtues of free enterprise in front of the logo, G.E., along with Westinghouse, Allis-Chalmers and other giant corporations, was habitually controlling the market by clandestine price fixing and bid rigging agreements, all of which led, in 1960, to grand jury indictments, in what was characterized by the Justice Department as the largest criminal case ever brought under the Sherman Anti-Trust Act," Doctorow noted.

As a child I watched Reagan pitch the joys of 20-mule team Borax on Death Valley Days, two reoccurring themes on the Old West show were the joys of imperialist conquest and genocide against indigenous people. All of it was served up by the smiley-faced Gipper. Bertrand Gross would later assess the Reagan administration as "friendly fascism."

Caught up in the Goldwater conservative movement, Reagan realized that he could deliver the right-wing reactionary script better than the much more intellectual Senator from Arizona. Thus, in 1966, Reagan took his highly-honed hokum and became the ultimate shill for the far right. As the New Republic pointed out during his 1966 campaign for Governor of California, "Reagan is anti-labor, anti-Negro, anti-intellectual, anti-planning, anti-20th century." Reagan campaigned against the civil rights movement, the peace movement, the student rights movement and the Great Society. In his fantasy world, Reagan equated giant price-fixing corporations with small town entrepreneurs. As every long-hair in the late 60s knew, Ronald Reagan was "the drugstore truck-drivin' man, the head of the Ku Klux Klan." He said if the students at Berkeley wanted a bloodbath, he would give them one. James Rector was shot dead soon after.

The real legacy of Reagan can be found in Philadelphia, Mississippi where he announced his candidacy for the Presidency in 1980. Previously, the most important political event in Philadelphia had been the deaths of civil rights workers, Andrew Goodman, Michael Schwerner and James Cheney in 1964. Reagan appeared, sans hood, to talk in those well-known racist code words about "state's rights." This was no mistake or misunderstanding. Reagan was signaling the right-wing movement that he would carry their racist agenda. Remember in 1984, his political operatives accused Walter Mondale of being "a San Francisco-style Democrat."

Reagan reached out and embraced the racist apartheid government of South Africa through his policy of so-called "constructive engagement." Reagan's solution to the de-industrialization of America was to build the prison industrial complex. His centerpiece was a racist so-called "War on Drugs" while his friends in the CIA used narcotics peddlers as "assets." And then Reagan's El Salvadorian Contra buddies began bringing in crack.

Reagan's response to the 1981-1982 recession, the worst economic downturn since the Great Depression, was to declare ketchup a vegetable, release federal cheese surpluses, and shackle the strike leaders of the air traffic control union hand and foot and lead them off to jail. My most pronounced memories of the Reagan years are the three hour cheese line and the German care packages to unemployed workers in Detroit.

In the first two years of the Reagan administration, his policy was a forced economic recession and de-industrialization of the United Stated. He cut federal low income housing funds by 84%; his tax cuts for the rich, his "trickle-on" the poor and working class economics ended up tripling all previously existing U.S. government debt. So, when I think of the Reagan legacy, I think of urban decay, crack, homelessness, racism, rampant corporatism and the destruction of the American dream. Amidst the growing homelessness and despair, I remember seeing graffiti all over inner-city Detroit that simply said: "Ronald Wilson Reagan 666." Reagan's policies so marked him as "the beast" in Detroit, blue-collar workers actually cheered when he was shot. The hottest song on underground radio was "Hinckley had a Vision." The song's refrain, "He knew, he knew."

When the mainstream media was analyzing Reagan's legacy and actively participating in the mythologizing of the 40th president, they conveniently ignored volumes of work by mainstream reporters. Wall Street Journal reporter Jane Mayer and Los Angeles Times reporter Doyle McManus documented Reagan's diminishing mental capacity in Landslide:

In March 1987 a memo was written by Jim Cannon to Howard Baker, Reagan's new Chief of Staff. His first recommendation: "Consider the possibility that section four of the 25th amendment might be applied." The amendment allows for the removal of the president when "the president is unable to discharge the powers and duties of his office." Mayer and McManus reported that staffers told Cannon in confidence that Reagan had become "inattentive and inept ... He was lazy; he wasn't interested in the job ... he wouldn't read the papers they gave him - even short position papers and documents ... he wouldn't come over to work - all he wanted to do was watch movies and television at the residence." Scholarly works have been written on Reagan's confusion of facts with Hollywood images.

The problem with the great communicator was the content of his messages. Reagan was a paid shill of the plutocrats, who used his charm and acting skills to hawk, like soap, mean spirited social policies and sell a fantasy version of the American Dream to common folk that trusted him.

June 16, 2004

REMEMBERING REAGAN

WASSERMAN

Those who hate "liberals" really hate a free America

The rightist "conservative" media moguls who hate "liberals" actually hate a free America.

Rush Limbaugh and Ann Coulter,   Hannity and O'Reilly, the Weekly Standard and Wall Street Journal---they all rant at some unspecified species allegedly left of center.

But right from its birth, America has been the very definition of a liberal nation.

Today's Foxist ditto-heads would have hated all America's founders: Franklin, Washington, Jefferson, Madison, Adams, Paine, and even the father of the modern corporate state, Alexander Hamilton.

All were liberals, both classic and modern. The documents they wrote---the Declaration of Independence, the Constitution, the Bill of Rights---all were the definition of liberal. Rush's "conservative" rightists would have hated them then. And though they won't admit it, they hate them now.

As for ending slavery, Ann Coulter would have SCREAMED at Abe Lincoln. The Emancipation Proclamation would have INFURIATED Hannity. The Gettysburg Address would have ENRAGED O'Reilly.

And don't even MENTION the environmentalism of U.S. Grant or Teddy Roosevelt.

But lets start with Ben Franklin, the true father of our country. This ultimate Enlightenment genius was the western world's most famous citizen. The man who defined electricity was America's leading writer, publisher, diplomat and humorist. "Poor Richard's Almanac" was one of the world's most influential publications. Franklin helped found so many institutions---public libraries, post offices, insurance companies---and made so many inventions---like the lightning rod and Franklin stove---that his vita fills whole books.

He was the only man to sign the Big Three: The Declaration, the Treaty of Paris (which sealed the Revolution's victory) and the Constitution.

Ben Franklin was also the ultimate liberal. He signed the first abolitionist petition to Congress. Supremely tolerant, he loved beautiful women, fine food, and the French. He believed in freedom, diversity, the Enlightenment, and progress. He spoke with amusement of the wild oats he sowed as a youth, and of "the ladies" he courted while seducing France into helping the young America free itself from the British.

Can you hear Rush's blood boil? Can you taste Ann Coulter's venom spewing through the centuries?

Then there's Tom Jefferson: brilliant, learned, master architect, ultimate phrase turner, Lockean liberal. Nobody stoked the leftist rhetoric of revolution and democracy, equality and progress better than Jefferson. He was a slave-owner, which the right would have liked. But he also consorted with one, the spirited Sally Hemmings, with whom he had at least three children. Can you hear Jerry Falwell SCREAM!!!

Then that shrimpy James Madison, spouting off about human liberties, combing the state constitutions to draft that ultimate liberal screed, the Bill of Rights. Hannity would have declared it "obsolete" at birth. If there's one document the conservatives hate most of all, it's Jamie Madison's Ten Commandments of civil rights and liberty.

Even George Washington, the ultimate war hero, stood his ground on a free America. When offered the dictatorship, he refused, saying America should remain a republic. Can you imagine George Bush, who never saw battle, doing the same?

To top it off, the master of Mount Vernon took enormous pains to make sure his slaves were freed and well cared for upon his death. What a bleeding heart!

As for Hamilton, the darling of the early corporations was born a bastard. He was a monarchist, which the National Review would have liked. He set the foundation for the modern American industrial state, from which Murdoch still profits.

But like Bill Clinton, Hamilton was also forced to admit to an extra-marital affair. And---can you believe it---he was an abolitionist! He opposed slavery!! Fox News is howling!!!

Even John Adams, staunch federalist, distruster of the people, supported the Bill of Rights. When Haitian slaves staged the world's second anti-imperial revolution, Adams stood by them. He even made national headlines by having a man of color to dinner! The Wall Street Journal edit page would have gone ballistic!

And that feminist wife of his, that Hillary ....er Abigail Adams. Rush would have branded her the ultimate femi-nazi.

Throw in Abe Lincoln, that liberal ACLU-type lawyer, fighting a war to free black people, telling the southerners they can't secede. A damn totalitarian, right O'Reilly?

Then U.S. Grant, who established Yellowstone Park, and Teddy Roosevelt who fought for so many more like it. Wimps! Greenies!! Bleeding hearts!!! Eco-Terrorists!!!!

Put it all together and you have a group of pointy-headed liberal geniuses whose Declaration of Independence, Constitution, Bill of Rights, Emancipation Proclamation, national parks and much much more remain the liberal bulwark of world freedom---unless the America-haters can destroy them. Unless the new George III can use the sword of terror to stab America's liberal heart.

The word "Christian" does not appear in the Constitution, no matter what Pat Robertson says. Most of the founders were Deists. They believed a divine being set this world in motion and then set the laws of nature free to work their magic.

Most of all the Founding Fathers hated---UNANIMOUSLY--- the idea of an official church, or a bunch of self-appointed bigots telling everyone else what to believe.

They bitterly opposed theocrats like Falwell and Robertson who forever preach that those who question the corporate church-state are traitors. In the Foxist world, diversity itself is intolerable.

But it was precisely that diversity the Founding Fathers wrote the Bill of Rights to protect.

In short, they were LIBERALS. And the nation they so successfully spawned has always been just that---LIBERAL.

So when we hear extremists like Limbaugh and Coulter, Hannity and O'Reilly howling away, we know it's not just liberals they hate. It's the free, diverse, tolerant nation the Founding Fathers created. The one whose liberal Bill of Rights lets even Foxist America-haters make oxy-morons of themselves all day, everyday.

That's how Ben and Tom and his liberal pals wanted it. May it always be thus.

June 1, 2004

Before   **After**

WASSERMAN

On the anniversary of defeat in Vietnam, it's once again about an empire getting its butt kicked

Thirty years after defeat in Vietnam, while the mainstream media contorts itself with oil-free justifications for the Bush attack on Iraq, George Will speaks clearly.

An administration that does not believe in democracy is not in Iraq to impose democracy.

It is there, says Will, to maintain the empire. Yes, he's used the E word and is proud of it.

But what he doesn't say is that the empire is in the process of getting its butt kicked. Again. The mainstream debate is now about whether or not the US should have gotten into Iraq, and how to maintain its presence.

But few are facing the reality that when the US finally leaves Iraq---and it will---in defeat and disgrace, its personnel are likely to be fleeing embassy rooftops by helicopter, yanked skyward as desperately as in Saigon on this day in 1975.

The George Wills and George Bushes of the world will blame

how it can achieve its ends there are ultimately beside the point. With more US soldiers killed this April than died overthrowing Saddam in the first place, the slaughter has barely begun. Imperial warplanes pour down fire Guernica-style on unseen civilian-soldiers in Fallujah while devastating and infuriating the civilian population. The spectacle of blind, blundering bloodshed can only escalate. The US scurries the streets with a big bull's eye painted on its back.

This war is over. The mopping up has begun---by the Iraqis. The hatred of we Americans by the people we have attacked far exceeds what we experienced in Vietnam. There, they admired our Constitution, our Bill of Rights, our democratic core.

Today, the most cynical and effective enemy of those sacred American values sits ignorant and unelected in the White House. Why would the Iraqis or anyone else believe the US is waging war to bring them democracy while it crusades to crush it at home?

And why would we grace the argument over how many troops we should send at what cost when what's left of our army is drowning in a nation that wants us gone.

Theodore Roosevelt, the founder of the modern American empire, famously advised to "Speak softly and carry a big stick."

But his malapropic progeny George W. Bush can barely speak at all. Bush will never admit that the big stick of Empire has shattered in Baghdad. Or that every minute US troops stay there only makes things worse, with no tangible payback in sight, only the twisted prospect of yet another rooftop exit.

April 30, 2004

WHITE HOUSE INTELLIGENCE BRIEFING

WASSERMAN

Oscar smiles on "Fog of War" and its warnings on Iraq

Even on Oscar night, the war in Vietnam still rages. With a billion people glued to their tubes, the old battle cry that "the whole world is watching" was once again true.

As "Fog of War" won Sunday night for best documentary, we have an AWOL president prancing in a flight suit he did not earn, and a Democratic front-runner who was a hero on both sides an issue that still deeply divides us.

Most recently we've also had "The Quiet American," a stunning portrayal of how the US actually got into that horrible war. Behind them both loom the ghosts of three men: John F. Kennedy, Lyndon Johnson and the centerpiece of "Fog of War, Robert McNamara.

Kennedy is still with us because we don't know what he would have done. Bitter disputes still rage over the meaning of his withdrawal of 1000 (of 16,000) advisors just before his death, and his pledge to be out of Vietnam in 1965. Angry lawsuits have flared up---and could again---over whether Lyndon Johnson was misled, who might have done it, and why he escalated that catastrophic war in an unparalleled act of individual, party and national suicide.

But the real roots of this conflict come from the Cold War. "The

Quiet American" is as brilliant a book about the era's folly as has ever been written. Graham Greene's graceful, understated portrait of the prototypical young CIA operative who blunders around 1952 Saigon like a buffalo in heat is a multi-layered classic that will last through the ages. The Oscar-honored film adaptation does it justice. Michael Caine is brilliant as the weathered Brit making his last journalistic stand in the distant provinces. He has gone native and has burned his bridges behind him. Brendan Fraser brings him the war he needs to justify the outpost. As a cocky, Harvard-style imperial missionary, Fraser shows us how imperial America decided it could and would tell the Vietnamese and the rest of the Third World how they would be governed. With his Boy Scout handbook on installing non-communist regimes, he sounds like an early neo-con explaining how things will be in Iraq. Though stockier and smarter, he conjures the frat boy George W. Bush running loose in the imperial tropics. Now in video/DVD, "The Quiet American" has its slow moments early on. But it's a stunning, essential portrayal of how we got into the quagmire that ruined this nation.

Robert McNamara's performance in "Fog of War" is equally essential, and follows on nicely. Clearly this is the octogenarian's mea culpa and farewell performance. Sharp, aggressive, brilliant, he did not sit for 20 hours of interview without purpose.

Ironically, the greatest shocks come with his discussion of his role in World War II. Instrumental in the fire bombing of Tokyo at the end of World War II, he almost casually admits to being a war criminal. He adds, with a line for the ages, the deciding factor in what constitutes a war crime is which side won the war.

But since that was the "Good War," McNamara knows he can be forgiven. In Vietnam, we lost, and things are more delicate.

This film from Errol Morris is very slickly produced. The music from Philip Glass is hypnotic, and the quick-step use of graphics is imaginative.

But the packaging---and lack of balancing counter-narrative---produces some shocking moments. For example, McNamara tells us that when told Vietnamese Premier Diem had been murdered,

JFK turned ashen. The implication is that the killing came as a surprise.

But JFK knew full well that planning for a coup was in motion, and must also have known that there was a likelihood Diem would be killed. Indeed, US Ambassador Henry Cabot Lodge offered Diem "safe passage" as the overthrow unfolded. And he cabled Kennedy to say "the prospects now are for a shorter war" soon after the murder.

McNamara's assertion that JFK was upset when news arrived of Diem's death has been repeated by General Maxwell Taylor in Stanley Karnow's excellent history of the Vietnam War. But the story, with its fungible explanations, could be cover. And JFK's infamous ambivalence and angst are still the source of excruciating debate about what he did and might have done in southeast Asia.

In retrospect Kennedy's own close-on death seems almost divine retribution for that ill-conceived murder. While one may disbelieve that JFK would have done otherwise, it is clear from then on that Lyndon Johnson prosecuted the war with the belief that it had to be won. The portrayal of Vietnam as Lyndon Johnson's war is widely shared.

McNamara is widely quoted as telling LBJ the war couldn't be won, and is happy to repeat the sentiment here. But key is that he never said it SHOULDN'T be won. And toward film's end he offers yet another shocking dissemblance. At a "reunion" dinner between former American and Vietnamese adversaries, McNamara says he almost "came to blows" with a counterpart who told him the Vietnamese were fighting for their independence, and not as part of the international communist conspiracy.

Here the scenario is almost laughable. Most of the world not hypnotized by American television knew quite well that the Vietnamese had been fighting for their independence for a thousand years. They fought the Chinese, the Japanese, the French, the Americans. And after the Americans, they fought the Chinese yet again.

For us to swallow what McNamara says happened at that dinner we would have to believe he knew absolutely nothing about

Vietnamese history. He apparently means to imply that somehow this horrible war was a just frightful, tragically avoidable misunderstanding.

Oh, please!

In the postscripts we're reminded that McNamara went on to serve many years at the head of the World Bank. He was every bit the imperialist there, with a legendary disregard for home rule and ecological sanity. We come away believing that he may have made the right call in telling Kennedy and Johnson we couldn't win in Vietnam. But he never answers for why we were really there. Only a more complete discussion of his goals and "achievements" at the World Bank could give us that insight, and for that we'll have to await the outtakes. Maybe Errol Morris can put them on the DVD.

Meantime, by far the most frightening sequences of this film come in McNamara's pre-Vietnam discussions of the Cuban missile crisis. There's little that's new. But whatever one thinks of this man morally, there's no disputing his technical genius, or that of our young president at the time, and his brother. They faced all-out nuclear war and somehow didn't let it happen.

Fast forward to the crew currently in the White House and you have a genuinely terrifying reality. Vietnam was a horror show. And McNamara was a smart man whose value system did not include the heart or wisdom needed to pull us out of what those "Quiet Americans" got us into.

But he, like the makers of "The Fog of War," have the good sense to warn that we are now at the brink of a "rabbit hole" in southwest Asia not unlike the one that decimated us in southeast Asia.

And tragically, that earlier jungle quagmire didn't hold a candle to what the fundamentalist fanatics now running this country could do to the world in a complex confrontation involving real weapons of mass destruction. They need to go, soon. They need to be replaced with people that have McNamara's brains, but with a human value system to match. Or we could all be goners.

If there's a subtext message to these two films, and to all Americans in this election year, it's that we need a crew in

Washington with both brains and heart. Right now, at our great peril, neither is to be seen.

February 28, 2004

FITRAKIS & WASSERMAN

Fahrenheit 911 is Fair and Balanced

We've come to expect poisonous and unbalanced attacks from the paid far right propagandists denouncing Michael Moore's documentary "Fahrenheit 911." But more disturbing are the scolds from tepid moderate mainstream journalists who often fail to read their own newspapers.

New York Times columnist Nicholas D. Kristof attacks the film because "Moore hints that the real reason Bush invaded Afghanistan was to give his cronies a chance to profit by building an oil pipeline there." Kristof attacks Moore for even raising this issue,. But he conveniently ignores volumes of information readily available to back up Moore's claim.

Perhaps Kristof, like President Bush, refuses to read. At least that would explain why he missed the raging international debate surrounding the Bush administration's well-documented, then-secret oil negotiations with the Taliban in the summer of 2001.

The book FORBIDDEN TRUTH: U.S.-TALIBAN SECRET OIL DIPLOMACY AND THE FAILED HUNT FOR BIN LADEN was an international bestseller. Written by French Intelligence experts Jean-Charles Brisard and Guillaume Dasquié, the book asserts that the Bush administration threatened the Taliban with the now-infamous words: "Either you accept our carpet of gold or we'll carpet you with bombs." The threat was made about a month before the attack on the World Trade Center and the Pentagon.

Kristof and his ilk prefer the simple-minded version offered by President Bush: the Taliban and Al Qaeda hate our freedom and liberty. That the world's largest military power in search of new oil supplies for the 21st century would threaten carpet bombing is something the mainstream corporate media simply refuses to consider.

Kristof also ignores the fact that the U.S. government installed Unocal advisor Harmid Karzai as the President of Afghanistan and provided him U.S. Special Forces as his praetorian guard. Moore mentions this in the film, but Kristof leaves it out of his column, saying the "Administration's huge errors aren't because of deceit." But that statement itself is very deceitful.

Kristof also fails to acknowledge National Security Advisor Zbigniew Brzezinski's THE GRAND CHESSBOARD. Brzezinski calmly outlines a thesis that U.S. domination of the globe in the 21st century depends on its control of Central Asian oilfields. He also says the American public would not back an attack unless there was a terrorist attack that galvanized public opinion to seize the foreign oil.

Tom Teepen, syndicated columnist for the Cox New Service suggests that "Fahrenheit 911 is a polemic, not a documentary." Teepen says Moore "weaves conspiracy theories in part by conveniently leaving out key information."

Teepen belongs to that most despicable class of columnists known as "coincidence theorists." He also doesn't understand the true meaning of "polemic."

F9/11 opens with the 2000 election debacle in Florida. Moore could have recited from the U.S. Commission on Civil Rights, which documented that 54% of the rejected ballots in Florida were cast by black voters and 93% of African-Americans voted for Gore nationwide. The government report singled out George's brother Governor Jeb Bush, and the Bush brothers' close friend and Republican ally, Katherine Harris, for blame.

Moore could have presented investigative journalist Gregory Palast's reports for the BBC documenting that at least 58,000 eligible voters in Florida were denied the right to vote because their names were the same or similar to a felon.

Moore could have shown footage of a roadblock and told how Florida law enforcement officers turned black drivers of vans and buses away from the polls for failure to provide limousine or chauffer licenses.

Moore could have detailed how 20,000 Gore votes mysteriously disappeared in Volusia County and were later reinstated. That gap allowed Fox News analyst John Ellis to project his first cousin, G. W. Bush, to be the winner.

What else did Moore leave out?:

In his AMERICAN DYNASTY, Republican theorist Kevin Philips documents four generations of Bush family war profiteers dating back to World War I. This includes Samuel Bush's dual role as entrepreneur with Buckeye Steel Casting and government official on the Armaments Board.

George W. Bush's grandfather, Prescott Bush, was a key operative in the Union Banking Corporation that was seized by the U.S. government in 1942 and liquidated under the Trading with the Enemy Act for helping fund the Nazi war effort. Granddaddy Bush joined the Board of Directors of Union Bank in 1934 and stayed there as the bank aided Hitler's rise to power. The government liquidation yielded a reported $750,000 apiece for Prescott Bush and his father-in-law, George Herbert Walker.

The Bush family is close friends of the self-proclaimed Messiah and creepy cult leader Reverend Sun Myung Moon. In January 1995, Moon's Women's Federation for World Peace paid Bush the Elder at least one million dollars for a speech. Former President Bush was also the principal speaker in the November 1996 opening dinner for Moon's new weekly newspaper "Tiempos del Mundo" of Argentina.

Pulitzer Prize winner Seymour Hersh reported in February 2002's New Yorker that the Bush administration authorized U.S. cooperation with Pakistan in the December 2001 "Kunduz airlift" that sent airplanes and helicopters to rescue Pakistanis fighting with the Taliban and Al Qaeda. Note that the Unocal pipeline from

Central Asia goes through Afghanistan into Pakistan. A coincidence?

Article VI of the Nuremberg Charter defines "Crimes Against Peace" as "planning, preparation, initiation or waging of war of aggression or war in violation of international treaties . . . or participation in a common plan or conspiracy . . . to wage an aggressive war." The Bush doctrine of "pre-emption" really had nothing to do with pre-empting an Iraqi attack on the U.S. It is simply the widely discredited Nazi doctrine of "preventive war" established by Hitler to claim the right to attack any country that may pose some possible threat at an unspecific time in the future.

FALSE PROFITS: THE INSIDE STORY OF BCCI, THE WORLD'S MOST CORRUPT FINANCIAL EMPIRE, by award-winning journalists Peter Truell and Larry Gurwin, documents in detail that Bush brothers Jeb and George both had close links to the drug-running Bank of Credit and Commerce International (aka "Bank of Crooks and Criminals International," according to the CIA).

Criminal and civil suits against BCCI establish that Bush's good buddy James R. Bath, was a close business associate of Osama bin Laden's brother-in-law, terrorist financier Khalid bin Mahfouz. Moore correctly shows that Bath and Bush were both disciplined by the Air National Guard at the same time.

Professor Katherine Van Wormer, co-author of the authoritative text ADDICTION TREATMENT, suggests that "George W. Bush manifests all the classic patterns of what alcoholics in recovery call 'the dry drunk.' His behavior fits a pattern of years of heavy drinking and possible cocaine use."

These are just a few facts that Michael Moore left out of his fair and balanced documentary Fahrenheit 9/11. Those who hate this moderate, well-documented film may be most bothered by the actual footage of President Bush. Key scenes include: Bush's infamous, endless study of MY PET GOAT in an elementary school class while the World Trade Center burned; Bush's legendary banquet speech referring to "the haves and have-mores" as "my base"; Bush's bumbling, malapropic final warning to "don't be fooled again."

What most bugs F911 critics is clearly not the material Michael Moore presents. It's the fair and balanced footage of George W. Bush revealing who he truly is.

July 15, 2004

ACCEPT THE LORD GOD'S DIVINE GIFT OF FREEDOM!

WASSERMAN

Replacing the irreplaceable Paul Wellstone

The memorial at Kent State University was the perfect place to walk and talk with Paul Wellstone. He was hurting from an old college wrestling injury, and perhaps, though we didn't know it then, from the onset of MS. So he could barely move around. But what walking he could do, he did with grace. An athlete in pain.

Paul was also, as always, sharp and committed. We were awaiting our turns to speak to an energetic band of young citizen activists, fresh out of college. They were bright, progressive environmentalists, full of vim and promise, a welcome island in the 1990s sea of Clintonian materialism.

As we circled the memorial we found ourselves close to tears. When this official butchery happened, we were both active in the movement against the war in Vietnam. The 1970 shooting, engineered by Richard Nixon and Ohio Gov. James A. Rhodes, sent a message: you could be killed.

We took it personally. The dead were our slightly younger compatriots. They were white, middle class innocents exercising their sacred American rights on the sanctuary of a college campus. The use of live ammunition by National Guardsmen not much older than the students they were killing was a horrifying breach of faith. The war had come home.

But in the mid 1990s, as we walked through the memorial and saw where the Guardsmen were when they fired, and where the students were when they fell, Paul and I had a different perspective. Now we felt it as parents, ingesting the heartsickness of what it must have meant to scrape together enough to send children to a state university only to see them gunned down with bullets paid for by our own tax dollars. An utterly terrifying hurt.

And now, soulsick again, we ask: how can we possibly replace Paul Wellstone? Paul's speech at Kent was, as always, full of fire. The son of immigrant Jews, he was an unabashed prairie populist. He preached the old-time grass roots religion. His unswerving belief in democracy and the basic wisdom of average people was a faith he alone carried into the US Senate until he was joined by Wisconsin's Russ Feingold, who was inspired by Paul to run.

Indeed, the idea that such a man could be in the US Senate seems an inherent impossibility. Today it is a body almost totally defined by money and the hollow rhetoric it buys. By contrast, Paul was grounded in the best realities of the American democratic tradition. His primary commitment was to the basics of social justice and human rights.

Paul's election campaigns also illustrated a lesson the Democratic Party seems incapable of learning. In 1996, in the midst of a tough re-election campaign, Wellstone voted against Bill Clinton's harsh, cynical welfare "reform" bill. Conventional wisdom said this would doom his re-election bid. But Paul's poll numbers immediately jumped, and he walked back into office.

This year, alone among Democrats in competitive races, Wellstone cast a principled vote against granting George Bush blanket war powers. Again, conventional wisdom said this would doom his campaign. Again his poll numbers leapt up, and his campaign took on the aspect of a winner.

The personal tragedy of Paul's fiery death, with his wife, his daughter, campaign aides and two pilots, is staggering. And so is the loss of Paul as a political player.

Aside from Feingold, whose style is far less emotional, Paul's commitments in the Senate were completely unique. He was willing to go to Colombia and shout against the injustice and brutality of the US "drug war" there. The issues of poverty, social injustice and racism stayed at the core of his being in a time when the smug essence of being a US Senator is about using the rhetoric of those issues as occasional window dressing. Paul genuinely believed in the need to save the environment, stop nuclear power and bring on an era of renewable energy, and he acted on those beliefs.

Wellstone's demise has further destabilized an already deeply troubled election. When Missouri's Mel Carnahan died in a plane crash in 2000, his name successfully remained on the ballot, and the Democratic governor filled the seat with Carnahan's wife, who is now fighting desperately to retain it.

In Minnesota, the governor is Jesse Ventura, and the situation is chaotic. The Democrats are hoping to replace Wellstone with the much more conservative Walter Mondale. Very importantly, Mondale might hold the seat, and thus help retain a Democratic edge in the Senate, preserving a crucial, tiny brake on the authoritarian power of the Bush regime.

But Walter Mondale is no Paul Wellstone. Someone tangible, on a day-to-day basis, has to pick up the physical work he did and do it just as well.

I know of one such instance. In 1995 the great George M. Barley died in a mysterious plane crash. George was a successful, much-loved businessman whose passion was to save the Florida Everglades. His ceaseless energy and effective brilliance seemed to make him the indispensable man in a brutal campaign against the entrenched power of Big Sugar. When he died, common wisdom said all that would end, and that the Everglades were hopelessly doomed.

But his wife Mary picked up the charge and has made George's legacy into a viable political reality. Helping to found a wide range of Save-the Everglades organizations, Mary led the campaign to win the nation's first "make the polluter pay" amendment to a state constitution. She was greatly responsible for federal legislation earmarking up to $8 billion to save the Everglades. She has become known far and wide as the essential guardian of that irreplaceable natural treasure.

Tragically, the wonderful Sheila Wellstone died with Paul, along with their daughter. His sons may yet have their day. But ultimately, Paul showed that with virtually no money, and a whole lot of spunk and commitment, individuals can change the world. Paul chose to do that, against all odds, by somehow getting into the US Senate, and then keeping the faith once there.

Paul inspired Russ Feingold to do much the same in winning a Senate seat in neighboring Wisconsin. Feingold then joined John McCain to win the first battle in the long war for election finance reform. Hopefully that, in turn, could jar the door for others like Paul who might keep their commitment to actually serve the people who elect them.

Paul Wellstone now stands as a role model for those wanting to reclaim a political system thoroughly corrupted and debased by big money.

No one can personally replace this dear brother.

But we are obliged to try. The work he set out to do, the commitments he made, and the vacuum he left us to fill are as clear as the light in Paul's eyes when he shouted his passion to all who would listen.

October 30, 2002

Hey kids! it's the HOMELAND SECURITY JUNIOR ACTIVITY PAGE!!
Can you tell right from wrong below?!

Spot the mistakes in the White House!

We the People

HALLIBURTON

WORD SEARCH!
FIND THE WMD IN IRAQ!!

```
W M W M O I L M
M D W D M O I L
O I L W M I D W
D W M O I L M D
W O I L D W D M
M D W M O I L D
W M O I L W M W
O I L M D O I L
```

www.kirktoons.com KIRK

HELP THE WEARY TROOPS FIND THEIR WAY OUT OF IRAQ!!

↑ Afghanistan

← Bosnia

Kyrgyzstan →

South Korea ↓

COLOR THE EMPIRE'S NEW CLOTHES!

Help the administration CONNECT THE DOTS!

1. Hart-Rudman report
2. John O'Neil warnings
3. FAA warnings
4. Phoenix flight school memo
5. Moussaoui's interest in learning to fly, but to not land or take off
6. May 17 Presidential briefing
7. August 6 Presidential briefing
8. Whatever it is White House is hiding from 9-11 commission

2•   3• 6•   7•

1•   4• 5•   8•

Printed in the United States
27317LVS00006B/196-216